# A Philosopher's Journey

# A Philosopher's Journey

Essays from Six Decades

Steven M. Cahn

RESOURCE *Publications* • Eugene, Oregon

A PHILOSOPHER'S JOURNEY
Essays from Six Decades

Copyright © 2020 Steven M. Cahn. All rights reserved. Except for brief quotations in critical publications or reviews, no part of this book may be reproduced in any manner without prior written permission from the publisher. Write: Permissions, Wipf and Stock Publishers, 199 W. 8th Ave., Suite 3, Eugene, OR 97401.

Resource Publications
An Imprint of Wipf and Stock Publishers
199 W. 8th Ave., Suite 3
Eugene, OR 97401

www.wipfandstock.com

PAPERBACK ISBN: 978-1-7252-6791-6
HARDCOVER ISBN: 978-1-7252-6792-3
EBOOK ISBN: 978-1-7252-6793-0

Manufactured in the U.S.A.                    07/08/20

To my wife,
Marilyn Ross, M.D.

# Contents

*Preface* | ix

## PART I: Free Will | 1

1. Determinism and Freedom | 3
2. Random Choices | 18
3. Misunderstanding Fatalism | 21
4. Time, Truth, and Ability | 25
5. Does God Know the Future? | 33

## PART II: Religious Belief | 39

6. *The* Question: Plato's *Euthyphro* | 41
7. The Noes Have It: Hume's *Dialogues concerning Natural Religion* | 47
8. Philosophical Proofs and Religious Commitment | 54
9. The Problem of Evil and the Problem of Good | 58
10. Religion without God | 64

## PART III: Morality and Society | 73

11. John Dewey at Eighty | 75
12. Two Concepts of Affirmative Action | 85
13. Justifying Liberal Education | 97

## Part IV: Well-Being | 103

14. Happiness and Ignorance | 105
15. Maximizing Well-Being? | 108
16. Meaningful Lives | 111
17. How to View Death | 115

## Part V: Puzzles | 119

18. The Strange Case of John Shmarb | 121
19. The Divestiture Problem | 126
20. Two Lives | 128

*Sources* | *131*
*Works of Steven M. Cahn* | *133*
*About the Author* | *137*
*Index* | *139*

# Preface

In 2019 Wipf & Stock published *The Road Traveled and Other Essays*, a collection of my recent writings. For this companion volume I have chosen favorite philosophical articles from the 1960s to the present, reflecting my long-standing interests in the concept of free will, the rationality of religious belief, the insights of John Dewey, the affirmative action debate, the aims of higher education, and the nature of living well. Also included are several philosophical puzzles, a genre I have long enjoyed.

As might be expected, my work reflects the influences of my teachers, colleagues, and students. Sadly, virtually all my teachers and many of my colleagues have left the scene, and most of my former students (although happily not all) have disappeared from my view. Nevertheless, I have not forgotten how many of them contributed to my thinking.

I thank my brother, Victor L. Cahn, professor emeritus of English at Skidmore College, for his invaluable advice, stylistic and otherwise. And, as always, I am grateful to my wife, Marilyn Ross, MD. for more than I can put into words.

# PART I

## Free Will

# 1

## Determinism and Freedom

IN 1924 THE AMERICAN people were horrified by a senseless crime of extraordinary brutality. The defendants were eighteen-year-old Nathan Leopold and seventeen-year-old Richard Loeb, the sons of Chicago millionaires, and brilliant students who had led seemingly idyllic lives. Leopold was the youngest graduate in the history of the University of Chicago, and Loeb the youngest graduate in the history of the University of Michigan. Suddenly they were accused of the kidnapping and vicious murder of fourteen-year-old Bobby Franks, a cousin of Loeb's. Before the trial even began, Leopold and Loeb both confessed, and from across the country came an outcry for their execution.

The lawyer who agreed to defend them was Clarence Darrow, the outstanding defense attorney of his time. Because Leopold and Loeb had already admitted their crime, Darrow's only chance was to explain their behavior in such a way that his clients could escape the death penalty. He was forced to argue that Leopold and Loeb were not morally responsible for what they had done, that they were not to be blamed for their actions. But how could he possibly maintain that position?

Darrow's defense was a landmark in the history of criminal law. He argued that the actions of his clients resulted from hereditary and

## Part I: Free Will

environmental forces beyond their control.[1] Leopold suffered from a glandular disease that left him depressed and moody. Originally shy with girls, he had been sent to an all-girls school as a cure but had sustained deep psychic scars from which he never recovered. In addition, his parents instilled in him the belief that his wealth absolved him of any responsibility toward others. Pathologically inferior because of his diminutive size, and pathologically superior because of his wealth, he became an acute schizophrenic.

Loeb suffered from a nervous disorder that caused fainting spells. During his unhappy childhood, he had often thought of committing suicide. He was under the control of a domineering governess and was forced to lie and cheat to deceive her. His wealth led him to believe that he was superior to all those around him, and he developed a fascination for crime, an activity in which he could demonstrate his superiority. By the time he reached college he was severely psychotic.

In his final plea Darrow recounted these facts. His central theme was that Leopold and Loeb were in the grip of powers beyond their control, that they themselves were victims.

> I do not know what it was that made these boys do this mad act, but I do know there is a reason for it. I know they did not beget themselves. I know that any one of an infinite number of causes reaching back to the beginning might be working out in these boys' minds, whom you are asked to hang in malice and in hatred and in injustice, because someone in the past has sinned against them ... What had this boy to do with it? He was not his own father; he was not his own mother; he was not his own grandparents. All of this was handed to him. He did not surround himself with governesses and wealth. He did not make himself. And yet he is to be compelled to pay.[2]

---

1. The following information is found in Irving Stone, *Clarence Darrow for the Defense* (Garden City, NY: Doubleday, Doran, 1941), 384–91.

2. *Attorney for the Damned*, ed. Arthur Weinberg (New York: Simon and Schuster, 1957), 37, 65.

## Determinism and Freedom

Darrow's pleas was successful, for Leopold and Loeb escaped execution and were sentenced to life imprisonment. Although they had committed crimes and were legally responsible for their actions, the judge believed they were not morally responsible, for they had not acted freely.

If the line of argument that Darrow utilized in the Leopold-Loeb case is sound, then not only were Leopold and Loeb not to blame for what they had done, but no person is ever to blame for any actions. As Darrow himself put it, "We are all helpless."[3] But is Darrow's argument sound? In other words, does the conclusion follow from the premises, and are the premises true?

We can formalize his argument as follows:

Premise 1: No action is free if it must occur.

Premise 2: In the case of every event that occurs, antecedent conditions, known or unknown, ensure the event's occurrence.

Conclusion: Therefore no action is free.

Premise (1) assumes that an action is free only if it is within the agent's power to perform it and within the agent's power not to perform it. In other words, whether a free action will occur is up to the agent. If circumstances require the agent to perform a certain action or require the agent not to perform it, then the action is not free.

Premise (2) is the thesis known as *determinism*. Put graphically, it is the claim that if at any time a being knew the position of every particle in the universe and all the forces acting on each particle, then that being could predict with certainty every future event. Determinism does not presume such a being exists; the being is only imagined in order to illustrate what the world would be like if determinism were true.

Darrow's conclusion, which is supposed to follow from premises (1) and (2), is that no person has free will. Note that to have free will does not imply being free with regard to all actions, for only the mythical Superman is free to leap tall buildings at a single bound. But so long as at least some of an agent's actions are free, the agent is said to have free will. What Darrow's argument

---

3. Weinberg, 37.

purports to prove is that not a single human action that has ever been performed has been performed freely.

Does the conclusion of Darrow's argument follow from the premises? If premise (2) is true, then every event that occurs must occur, for its occurrence is ensured by antecedent conditions. Because every action is an event, it follows from premise (2) that every action that occurs must occur. But according to premise (1), no action is free if it must occur. Thus if premises (1) and (2) are true, it follows that no action is free—the conclusion of Darrow's argument.

Even granting that Darrow's reasoning is valid, that is, that the conclusion follows from the premises, we need not accept the conclusion of his argument unless we grant the truth of his premises. Should we do so?

*Hard determinism* is the view that both premises of Darrow's argument are correct. In other words, a hard determinist believes that determinism is true and that, as a consequence, no person has free will.[4] Determinists note that whenever an event occurs, we all assume that a causal explanation can account for the occurrence of the event. Suppose, for example, you feel a pain in your arm and are prompted to visit a physician. After examining you, the doctor announces that the pain has no cause, either physical or psychological. In other words, you are supposed to be suffering from an uncaused pain. On hearing this diagnosis, you would surely switch doctors. After all, no one may be able to discover the cause of your pain, but surely something is causing it. If nothing were causing it, you wouldn't be in pain. This same line of reasoning applies whether the event to be explained is a loud noise, a change in the weather, or an individual's action. If the event were uncaused, it wouldn't have occurred.

We may agree, however, that the principle of determinism holds in the vast majority of cases, yet doubt its applicability in the realm of human action. While causal explanations may be found

---

4. The expressions "hard determinism" and "soft determinism" were coined by William James in his essay "The Dilemma of Determinism," reprinted in *Essays on Faith and Morals* (Cleveland: World, 1962), 145–83.

for rocks falling and birds flying, people are more complex than rocks or birds.

The determinist responds to this objection by asking us to consider any specific action: for instance, your decision to read this book. You may suppose your decision was uncaused, but did you not wish to acquire information about philosophy? The determinist argues that your desire for such information, together with your belief that the information is found in this book, caused you to read. Just as physical forces cause rocks and birds to do things, so human actions are caused by desires and beliefs.

If you doubt this claim, the determinist can call attention to our success in predicting people's behavior. For example, a store owner who reduces prices can depend on increasing visits by shoppers; an athlete who wins a major championship can rely on greater attention from the press. Furthermore, when we read novels or see plays, we expect to understand why the characters act as they do, and an author who fails to provide such explanations is charged with poor writing. The similarity of people's reactions to the human condition also accounts for the popularity of the incisive psychological insights of a writer such as the seventeenth-century, French aphorist La Rochefoucald. We read one of his maxims, for instance, "When our integrity declines, our taste does also,"[5] and nod our heads with approval, but are we not agreeing to a plausible generalization about the workings of the human psyche?

Granted, people's behavior cannot be predicted with certainty, but the hard determinist reminds us that each individual is influenced by a unique combination of hereditary and environmental factors. Just as each rock is slightly different from every other rock, and each bird is somewhat different from every other bird, so human beings differ from each other. Yet just as rocks and birds are part of an unbroken chain of causes and effects, so human beings, too, are part of that chain. Just as a rock falls because it breaks off from a cliff, so people act because of their desires and beliefs. And just as a rock has no control over the wind that causes

---

5. *The Maxims of La Rochefoucauld*, trans. Louis Kronenberger (New York: Random House, 1959), #379.

it to break off, so people have no control over the desires and beliefs that cause them to act. In short, we are said to have no more control over our desires and beliefs than Leopold and Loeb had over theirs. If you can control your desire for food and your friend cannot, the explanation is that your will is of a sort that can control your desire, and your friend's will is of a sort that cannot. That your will is of one sort and your friend's will of another is not within the control of either of you. As hard determinist John Hospers wrote, "If we can overcome the effects of early environment, the ability to do so is itself a product of the early environment. We did not give ourselves this ability; and if we lack it we cannot be blamed for not having it."[6]

At this point in the argument an anti-determinist is apt to call attention to recent developments in physics that have been interpreted by some thinkers as a refutation of determinism. They claim that work in quantum mechanics demonstrates that certain subatomic events are uncaused and inherently unpredictable. Yet some physicists and philosophers of science argue that determinism has not been refuted, because the experimental results can be understood in causal terms.[7] The outcome of this dispute, however, is irrelevant to the issue of human freedom, because the events we are discussing are not subatomic, and indeterminism on that level is compatible with the universal causation of events on the much larger level of human action.

Here, then, is a summary of hard determinism. According to this view, determinism is true and no person has free will. Every event that occurs is caused to occur, for otherwise why would it occur? Your present actions are events caused by your previous desires and beliefs, which themselves are accounted for by hereditary and environmental factors. These are part of a causal chain extending back far beyond your birth, and each link in the chain

---

6. John Hospers, "What Means This Freedom?" *Determinism and Freedom in the Age of Modern Science*, ed. Sidney Hook (New York: Collier, 1961), 138.

7. For a detailed discussion of the philosophical implications of quantum mechanics, see Ernest Nagel, *The Structure of Science* (New York: Harcourt Brace Jovanovich, 1961), ch. 10.

determines the succeeding link. Because you obviously have no control over events that occurred before your birth, and because these earlier events determined the latter ones, what follows is that you have no control over your present actions. In sum, you do not have free will.

The hard determinist's argument may appear plausible, yet few of us are inclined to accept its shocking conclusion. We opt, therefore, to deny one of its two premises. *Soft determinism* is the view that the conclusion is false because premise (1) is false. In other words, a soft determinist believes both that determinism is true and that human beings have free will. The implication of the position is that an action may be free even if it is part of a causal chain extending back to events outside the agent's control. While at first this view may appear implausible, it has been defended throughout the centuries by many eminent philosophers, including David Hume and John Stuart Mill.

An approach employed explicitly or implicitly by many soft determinists has come to be known as *the paradigm-case argument*. Consider it first in another setting, where its use is a classic of philosophical argumentation.

In studying physics, we learn that ordinary objects like tables and chairs are composed of sparsely scattered, minute particles. This finding may lead us to suppose that such objects are not solid. As physicist Sir Arthur Eddington put it, a "plank has no solidity of substance. To step on it is like stepping on a swarm of flies."[8]

Eddington's view that a plank is not solid was forcefully attacked by philosopher L. Susan Stebbing. She pointed out that the word *solid* derives its meaning from examples such as planks.

> For "solid" just is the word we use to describe a certain respect in which a plank of wood resembles a block of marble, a piece of paper, and a cricket ball, and in which each of these differs from a sponge, from the interior of a soap-bubble, and from the holes in a net . . . The point is that the common usage of language enables us to

---

8. A. S. Eddington, *The Nature of the Physical World* (New York: Macmillan, 1928), 342.

attribute a meaning to the phrase *a solid plank*; but there is no common usage of language that provides a meaning for the word *solid* that would make sense to say that the plank on which I stand is not solid.[9]

In other words, a plank is a paradigm case of solidity. Anyone who claims that a plank is not solid does not know how the word *solid* is used in the English language. Note that Stebbing was not criticizing Eddington's scientific views but only the manner in which he interpreted them.

The paradigm-case argument is useful to soft determinists, for in the face of the hard determinist's claim that no human action is free, soft determinists respond by pointing to a paradigm case of a free action, for instance, a person walking down the street. They stipulate that the individual is not under the influence of drugs, is not attached to ropes, is not sleepwalking, and so on; in brief, they refer to a normal, everyday instance of a person walking down the street. Soft determinists claim that the behavior described is a paradigm case of a free action, clearly distinguishable from instances in which a person is, in fact, under the influence of drugs, attached to ropes, or sleepwalking. These latter cases are not examples of free actions, or at best problematic examples, while the case the soft determinists cites is clear and seemingly indisputable. Indeed, according to soft determinists, anyone who claims that the act of walking down the street is not free does not know how the word *free* is used in English. Thus people certainly have free will, for we can cite obvious cases in which they act freely.

How do soft determinists define a *free action?* According to them, actions are free if the persons who perform them wish to do so and could, if they wished, not perform them. If your arm is forcibly raised, you did not act freely, for you did not wish to raise your arm. If you were locked in a room, you would also not be free, even if you wished to be there, for if you wished to leave, you couldn't.

Soft determinists emphasize that once we define *freedom* correctly, any apparent incompatibility between freedom and

9. L. Susan Stebbing, *Philosophy and the Physicists* (New York: Dover, 1958), 51–52.

determinism disappears. Consider some particular action I perform that is free in the sense explicated by soft determinists. Even if the action is one link in a causal chain extending far back beyond my birth, nevertheless I am free with regard to that action, for I wish to perform it, and if I did not wish to, I would not do so. This description of the situation is consistent with supposing that my wish is a result of hereditary and environmental factors over which I have no control. The presence of such factors is, according to soft determinists, irrelevant to the question of whether my action is free. I may be walking down a particular street because of my desire to buy a coat and my belief that I am heading toward a clothing store, and this desire and belief may themselves be caused by any number of other factors. But because I desire to walk down the street and could walk down some other street if I so desired, it follows that I am freely walking down the street. By this line of reasoning soft determinists affirm both free will and determinism, finding no incompatibility between them.

Soft determinism is an inviting doctrine, for it allows us to maintain a belief in free will without having to relinquish the belief that every event has a cause. Soft determinism, however, is open to serious objection.

The fundamental problem for soft determinists is that their definition of *freedom* is not in accord with the ordinary way in which we use the term. Note that soft determinists and hard determinists offer two different definitions of *freedom*. According to the hard determinist, an action is free if it is within my power to perform it and also within my power not to perform it. According to the soft determinist, an action is free if it is such that if I wish to perform it I can, and if I wish not to perform it I also can. To highlight the difference between these definitions, consider the case of a man who has been hypnotized and rolls up the leg of his pants as if to cross a stream. Is his action free? According to the hard determinist, the man's action is not free, for it is not within his power to refrain from rolling up the leg of his pants. According to the soft determinist's definition of *freedom*, the action would be considered free, for the agent desires to perform it, and if he didn't

## Part I: Free Will

desire to, he wouldn't. But a man under hypnosis is not free. Therefore the soft determinist's definition of *freedom* is unsatisfactory.

Perhaps this objection to soft determinism is unfair, because the desires of the hypnotized man are not his own but are controlled by the hypnotist. The force of the objection, however, is that the soft determinist overlooks whether a person's wishes or desires are themselves within that individual's control. The hard determinist emphasizes that my action is free only if it is up to me whether to perform it. But in order for an action to be up to me, I need to have control over my own wishes or desires. If I do not, my desires might be controlled by a hypnotist, a brainwasher, my family, hereditary factors, and so on, and thus I would not be free. Soft determinists do not appear to take such possibilities seriously, because, according to them, I would be free even if my desires were not within my control, so long as I was acting according to my desires and could act differently if my desires were different. But could my desires have been different? That is the crucial question. If my desires could not have been different, then I could not have acted in any way other than I did, which is the description of a person who is not free.

By failing to consider the ways in which a person's desires can be controlled by external forces beyond the individual's control, soft determinists offer a definition of *freedom* that I find not in accord with our normal use of the term. They may, of course, define terms as they wish, but we are interested in the concept of freedom relevant to questions of moral responsibility. Any concept of freedom implying that hypnotized or brainwashed individuals are morally responsible for their actions is not the concept in question.

What of the soft determinist's claim that a person's walking down the street is a paradigm case of a free action? Although I agree that the paradigm-case argument can sometimes be used effectively, the soft determinist's appeal to it does not seem convincing. To see why, imagine that we traveled to a land in which the inhabitants believed that every woman born on February 29 was a witch, and that every witch had the power to cause droughts. If we refused to believe that any woman was a witch, the philosophically

## Determinism and Freedom

sophisticated inhabitants might try to convince us by appealing to the paradigm-case argument, claiming that any woman born on February 29 is a paradigm case of a witch.

What would we say in response? How does this appeal to a paradigm case differ from Stebbing's appeal to a plank as a paradigm case of solidity? No one doubts that a plank can hold significant weight and is, in that sense, solid. But until women born on February 29 demonstrate the power to cause droughts and are, in that sense, witches, the linguistic claim alone has no force.

Are soft determinists appealing to an indisputable instance when they claim that a person's walking down the street is a paradigm case of a free action? Not at all, for as we saw in the trial of Leopold and Loeb, such apparently free actions may not turn out to be judged as free. By appealing to a disputable example as a paradigm case, soft determinists assume what they are supposed to be proving, the error known as *begging the question*. They are supposed to demonstrate that actions such as walking down the street are examples of free actions. Merely asserting that such actions are free is to overlook the hard determinist's argument that such actions are not free. No questionable instances can be used as a paradigm case, and walking down the street is, as Darrow demonstrated, a questionable example of a free action. Thus soft determinism has a serious weakness.

Remember that the hard determinist argues that because premises (1) and (2) of Darrow's argument are true, so is the conclusion. Soft determinists argue that premise (1) is false. If they are mistaken, then the only way to avoid hard determinism is to reject premise (2). That position is known as *libertarianism*.

The libertarian agrees with the hard determinist that if an action must occur, then it is not free. For the libertarian as well as for the hard determinist, I am free with regard to a particular action only if it is within my power to perform the action and within my power not to perform it.

But do persons ever act freely? The hard determinist believes that people are never free, because in the case of every action, antecedent conditions, known or unknown, ensure the action's

## Part I: Free Will

occurrence. Libertarians refuse to accept this conclusion but find it impossible to reject premise (1) of Darrow's argument. Therefore their only recourse is to reject premise (2). As Sherlock Holmes noted, "When you have eliminated the impossible, whatever remains, however improbable, must be the truth."[10] The libertarian thus denies that every event has a cause.

Why is the libertarian so convinced that people sometimes act freely? Consider an ordinary human action, for instance, raising your hand at a meeting to attract the speaker's attention. If you are attending a lecture and the time comes for questions from the audience, you believe it is within your power to raise your hand and also within your power not to. The choice is yours. Nothing forces you to ask a question, and nothing prevents you from asking one. What could be more obvious? If this description of the situation is accurate, then hard determinism is incorrect, for you are free with regard to the act of raising your hand.

The heart of the libertarian's position is that innumerable examples of this sort are conclusive evidence for free will. Indeed, we normally accept them as such. We assume on most occasions that we are free with regard to our actions, and, moreover, we assume that other persons are free with regard to theirs. If a friend agrees to meet us at six o'clock for dinner and arrives an hour late claiming to have lost track of time, we blame him for his tardiness, because we assume he had it within his power to act otherwise. All he had to do was glance at his watch, and assuming no special circumstances were involved, it was within his power to do so. He was simply negligent and deserves to be blamed, for he could have acted conscientiously. But to believe he could have acted in a way other than he did is to believe he was free.

How do hard determinists respond to such examples? They argue that such situations need to be examined in greater detail. In the case of our friend who arrives an hour late for dinner, we assume he is to blame for his actions, but the hard determinist points out that some motive impelled him to be late. Perhaps he was more

---

10. Sir Arthur Conan Doyle, *The Sign of Four*, in *The Complete Sherlock Holmes* (Garden City, NY: Doubleday, n.d.), 111.

interested in finishing his work at the office than in arriving on time for dinner. But why was he more interested in finishing his work than in arriving on time? Perhaps his parents had instilled in him the importance of work but not promptness. Hard determinists stress that whatever the explanation for his lateness, the motive causing it was stronger than the motive impelling him to arrive on time. He acted as he did because his strongest motive prevailed. Which motive was the strongest, however, was not within his control, and thus he was not free.

The hard determinist's reply may seem persuasive. How can I deny that I am invariably caused to act by my strongest motive? Analysis reveals, however, that the thesis is tautological, immune from refutation, and so devoid of empirical content. No matter what example of a human action is presented, a defender of the thesis could argue that the person's action resulted from the strongest motive. If I take a swim, taking a swim was my strongest motive. If I decide to forgo the swim and read a book instead, then reading a book was my strongest motive. How do we know that my motive to read a book was stronger than my motive to take a swim? Because I read a book and did not take a swim. If this line of argument appears powerful, the illusion will last only so long as we do not ask how we are to identify a person's strongest motive. The only possible answer appears to be that the strongest motive is the motive that prevails, the motive that causes the person to act. If the strongest motive is the motive causing the person to act, what force is in the claim that the motive causing a person to act is causing the person to act? No insight into the complexities of human action is obtained by trumpeting such a redundancy.

Thus the hard determinist does not so easily succeed in overturning the examples of free actions offered by the libertarian. However, both hard and soft determinists have another argument to offer against the libertarian's position. If the libertarian is correct that free actions are uncaused, why do they occur? Are they inexplicable occurrences? If so, to act freely would be to act in a random, chaotic, unintelligible fashion. Yet holding people morally blameworthy for inexplicable actions is unreasonable. If you

## Part I: Free Will

are driving a car and, to your surprise, find yourself turning the wheel to the right, we can hardly blame you if an accident occurs, for what happened was beyond your control.

Hence determinists argue that libertarians are caught in a dilemma. If we are caused to do whatever we do, libertarians assert we are not morally responsible for our actions. Yet if our actions are uncaused and inexplicable, libertarians again must deny our moral responsibility. How then can libertarians claim we ever act responsibly?

To understand the libertarian response, consider the simple act of a woman picking up a cell phone. Suppose we want to understand what she is doing and are told she is calling her stockbroker. The woman has decided to buy some stock and wishes her broker to place the appropriate order. With this explanation, we now know why this woman has picked up the phone. Although we may be interested in learning more about the woman or her choice of stocks, we have a complete explanation of her action, which turns out not to be random, chaotic, or unintelligible. We may not know what, if anything, is causing the woman to act, but we do know the reason for her action. The libertarian thus replies to the determinist's dilemma by arguing that an action can be uncaused yet understandable, explicable in terms of the agent's intentions or purposes.

Now contrast the libertarian's description of a particular action with a determinist's. Let the action be your moving your arm to adjust your radio. A determinist claims you were caused to move your arm by your desire to adjust the radio and your belief that you could make this adjustment by turning the dials. A libertarian claims you moved your arm in order to adjust the set.

Note that the libertarian explains human actions fundamentally differently from the way in which we explain the movement of rocks or rivers. If we speak of a rock's purpose in falling off a cliff or a river's purpose in flowing to the sea, we do so only metaphorically, for we believe that rocks and rivers have no purposes of their own but are caused to do what they do. Strictly speaking, a rock does not fall in order to hit the ground, and a river does not flow in order to reach the sea. Libertarians, however, are speaking not metaphorically but literally when they say that people act in order to achieve their purposes. After all, not even the most complex machine can act as a person does. A machine can break down and fail to operate, but only a human being can protest and stop work on purpose.

Is the libertarian's view correct? I doubt that anyone is justified in answering the question with certainty, but if the libertarian is right, human beings are often morally responsible for their actions. They deserve praise when acting admirably and blame when acting reprehensibly. Darrow may have been correct in arguing that Leopold and Loeb were not free agents, but if the libertarian is right, the burden of proof lay with Darrow, for he had to demonstrate that these boys were in that respect unlike the rest of us.

What if the libertarian is not correct? What if all human actions are caused by antecedent conditions, known or unknown, that ensure their occurrence? Moral responsibility would vanish, but even so people could be held legally responsible for their actions. Just as we need to be safeguarded against mad dogs, so we need protection from dangerous people. Thus even if no person were morally responsible, we would still have a legal system, courts, criminals, and prisons. Remember that Darrow's eloquence did not free his clients; indeed, he did not ask that they be freed. Although he did not blame them for their actions, he did not want those actions repeated. To Darrow, Leopold and Loeb were sick men who needed the same care as sick persons with a contagious disease. After all, in a world without freedom, events need not be viewed as agreeable; they should, however, be understood as necessary.

# 2

## Random Choices

THE LIBERTARIAN CLAIM THAT the doctrine of free will can be true only if determinism is false has often been attacked on the grounds that "what is random is no more free than what is caused."[1] As A. J. Ayer argued:

> Either it is an accident that I choose to act as I do or it is not. If it is an accident, then it is merely a matter of chance that I did not choose otherwise; and if it merely a matter of chance that I did not choose otherwise, it is surely irrational to hold me morally responsible for choosing as I did. But if it not an accident that I choose to do one thing rather than another, then presumably there is some causal explanation of my choice; and in that case we are led back to determinism.[2]

I want to call attention to a common phenomenon that has not often been the subject of philosophical concern but that on examination suggests that a random act, although seemingly uncaused, need be neither accidental or irresponsible.

We are frequently called on to make a conscious choice from among alternatives that are equal in their degree of attractiveness.

---

1. A. C. MacIntyre, "Determinism," *Mind* 66, no. 261 (1957), 30.
2. A. J. Ayer, *Philosophical Essays* (New York: St. Martin's Press, 1963), 275.

## Random Choices

"Pick a card." "Choose a number from one to ten." "Park your car in any of the available spaces." "Have a cupcake." Normally none of us has any difficulty making such a random choice. Yet how do we manage to perform these seemingly simple tasks? How do we decide which card to pick or which number to choose?

At a party you are offered a plate of cookies. You select one, and the following conversation ensues:

Host: "Why did you choose that one?"
You: "You said, 'Take one.' So I did."
Host: "But why did you take *that* one?"
You: "I don't know. I just chose."

At the store you buy one box of corn flakes rather than another of the same brand and size, although they appear equally wholesome. In the park you sit on one bench rather than another, although others would serve equally well. While writing a philosophical paper you choose "Jones" as an example of a proper name, although "Smith" would be equally appropriate. None of these decisions causes you any anguish; they are made with ease.

Can such random choices be explained? Of course, we can explain a person's deciding to spend money on corn flakes rather than prunes, although some philosophers would say such an explanation is ultimately causal in nature, while others would say the appropriate explanation is irreducibly in terms of the agent's reasons or purposes. But can we explain a person's decision to buy one particular box of corm flakes rather than another?

On the one hand, to suppose that each time I am asked to choose a box of cereal a causal explanation can be provided as to why I picked a certain one is to adhere to determinism but to extrapolate wildly beyond available empirical data. On the other hand, to assume the choice can be explained in terms of my intentions is to be committed to the view that if we have no reason to prefer one choice to another, then we cannot choose at all. Yet we have no trouble making a random choice even in circumstances in which we find it impossible, before or after, to think of any basis to prefer one of the alternatives. Indeed, if we had to postpone such a choice until we could figure out a reason for our preference, our

## Part I: Free Will

lives would come to a virtual standstill. Should I open this letter or that one first? Should I walk home this way or that?[3] Without the ability to make random choices, we would be caught in a nightmare of indecision.

I believe we possess the ability to make random choices. We are not condemned to the fate of Buridan's Ass, the animal featured in medieval debate who died while, equally pressed by hunger and thirst, he stood motionless midway between a bundle of hay and a pail of water. What we do in such a situation is make a random choice. Faced with equally attractive or unattractive alternatives, we are not bludgeoned into inactivity by some need for a decision principle. We simply choose. To refer to such a random choice as either accidental or irresponsible would surely be misleading.

P. H Nowell-Smith was thus mistaken when he equated a random occurrence with "an Act of God, or a miracle."[4] He even denied that such an occurrence could be an act at all, but, as we have seen, a random choice is an ordinary action that each of us performs frequently. Indeed, not only are random choices actions, they appear to be good candidates, although not the only ones, for membership in that class of actions we ordinarily designate as "free."

---

3. See William James's intriguing discussion of his choice whether to walk home by Divinity Avenue or Oxford Street in James, 155–57.

4. P. H. Nowell-Smith, *Ethics* (Baltimore: Penguin, 1954), 282.

# 3

# Misunderstanding Fatalism

MAJOR REFERENCE WORKS MISDESCRIBE fatalism, mistakenly rendering it vacuous or incoherent. The thesis, however, should not be dismissed out of hand.

For example, *The Oxford Dictionary of Philosophy*, Third Edition, contains the following entry: "[F]atalism: The doctrine that what will be will be, or that human action has no influence on events. 'Either a bullet has my number on it or it does not; if it does, then there is no point taking precautions for it will kill me anyhow; if it does not then there is no point taking precautions for it is not going to kill me; hence either way there is no point taking precautions.' The dilemma ignores the highly likely possibility that whether the bullet has your number on it depends on whether you take precautions. Fatalism is wrongly confused with determinism, which by itself carries no implications that human action is ineffectual."[1]

The first definition offered is a tautology, "what will be will be"; if that thesis is fatalism, then the doctrine is true but uninteresting. The second definition, "human action has no influence on events," is clearly false, because, for example, obtaining a divorce logically requires getting married. Examples like that of the bullet

---

1. Simon Blackburn, "Fatalism," *Oxford Dictionary of Philosophy*, Third Edition (New York and Oxford: Oxford University Press, 2016), 175.

## Part I: Free Will

were known in antiquity as the "idle argument," and the appropriate reply, given by the Stoic logician Chrysippus, is that taking precautions may save you, and, if so, then they were fated to do so. Hence such examples provide no refutation of fatalism. Furthermore, the difference between fatalism and determinism is not that fatalism claims human action is ineffectual but that fatalism makes no reference to causation. Moreover, some determinists affirm free will, but all fatalists deny it.

The entry for "fatalism" in *The Oxford Companion to Philosophy*, New Edition, is no more helpful.

> [F]atalism: The belief, not to be confused with causal determinism, that deliberation and action are pointless because the future will be the same no matter what we do. According to the famous "idle argument" of antiquity, "If it is fated for you to recover from this illness, you will recover whether you call in a doctor or not; similarly, if it is fated for you not to recover from this illness, you will not recover whether you call in a doctor or not; and either your recovery or non-recovery is fated; therefore there is no point in calling in a doctor." Thus all actions and choices are "idle" because they cannot affect the future. Determinists reject fatalism on the grounds that it may be determined that we can be cured only by calling the doctor.[2]

Here fatalism is identified with the "idle argument," as though that piece of reasoning is itself the fatalistic position. In fact, the "idle argument" is a supposed refutation of fatalism, easily answered with the response of Chrysippus that, for example, whether your call a doctor is as fated as whether you recover.

*The Cambridge Dictionary of Philosophy*, Third Edition, offers no entry on "fatalism" but refers readers to an article titled "free will problem." There the term "fatalism" is not mentioned, but the detailed discussion of free will and determinism includes the following two sentences: "Logical versions of determinism

---

2. Roy Weatherford, "Fatalism," *The Oxford Companion to Philosophy*, New Edition, ed. Ted Honderich (New York and Oxford: Oxford University Press, 2005), 291.

## Misunderstanding Fatalism

declare each future event to be determined by what is already true, specifically by the truth that it will occur then. Certain theological variants accept the *predestination* of all circumstances and events by a divine being who knows in advance that they will obtain."[3]

The term "logical determinism" suggests that fatalism is a form of determinism, which it is not. Furthermore, while divine foreknowledge can raise speculation about human freedom, fatalism does not rest on theism.

*The Routledge Encyclopedia of Philosophy* adds to the confusion. Its entry states: "'Fatalism' is sometimes used to mean the acceptance of determinism, along with a readiness to accept the consequence that there is no such thing as human freedom. The word is also often used in connection with a theological question: whether God's supposed foreknowledge means that the future is already fixed. But it is sometimes explained very differently, as the view that human choice and action have no influence on future events, which will be as they will be whatever we think or do. On the face of it this is barely coherent, and invites the assessment that fatalism is simply an expression of resigned acceptance."[4]

Here fatalism is first conflated with determinism, next misleadingly associated with a belief in God's foreknowledge, then equated with the tautology that what will be will be, and finally supposedly refuted by the "idle argument." The brief accompanying article begins by asserting that "Taken as meaning exactly what it says, the dictum that human choice and action have no influence on future events is absurd." This assertion is an example of the fallacy of *ignoratio elenchi,* arguing against a claim not in dispute.

Fortunately, the proper understanding of fatalism can be found in the *Encyclopedia of Ethics,* Second Edition. There the extended entry "fate and fatalism" authored by John Martin Fischer begins: "Fatalism can be understood as the doctrine that it is a

---

3. Tomas Kapitan, "Free Will Problem," *The Cambridge Dictionary of Philosophy,* Third Edition, ed. Robert Audi (Ne York: Cambridge University Press, 2015), 381–83.

4. Edward Craig, "Fatalism," *Routledge Encyclopedia of Philosophy.* ed. Edward Craig (London and New York: Routedge, 1998), vol. 3, 563–64.

logical or conceptual truth that agents are never free to do other than what they actually do."[5]

Note the following key points in Fischer's definition. First, fatalism is not a form of determinism. Second, fatalism does not presume theism. Third, fatalism denies free will. Fourth, fatalism does not affirm or imply that human actions have no influence on future events.

In sum, fatalism is not a tautology, a theological tenet, or a preposterous claim about the ineffectiveness of human action. Rather it is a challenging thesis denying free will on the basis of conceptual considerations and requiring for its assessment a careful exploration of issues regarding time, logic, and freedom.

---

5. John Martin Fischer, "Fate and Fatalism," *Encyclopedia of Ethics*, Second Edition, eds. Lawrence C. Becker and Charlotte B. Becker (New York and London: Routledge, 2001), 526–28.

# 4

## Time, Truth, and Ability
*CO-AUTHORED WITH RICHARD TAYLOR*

WE SHALL HERE BE concerned with statements of the form "$M$ does $A$ at $t$," wherein $M$ designates a specific person, $A$ a specific action, and $t$ a specific time. We shall refer to these as R-statements. Thus, "Someone raised his hand at noon last Tuesday," "Stilpo raised his hand," and "Stilpo did something at noon last Tuesday" are not R-statements; but "Stilpo raised his right hand at noon last Tuesday" is an R-statement.

Let us assume that it sometimes at least makes sense to speak of an agent's being able to render an R-statement true, as distinguished, for example, from simply *discovering* that it is true; and similarly, that it sometimes makes sense to speak of a person's being able to render an R-statement false. Thus Stilpo could render it true that he is running at a certain time simply by running at that time, and this would be something quite different from his then merely discovering—observing, noting, etc.—that he is running. He could, of course, render the same statement false in a variety of ways—by standing still, for instance, or by lying down, and so on. We, on the other hand, could not in any similar way render *that* R-statement true. We could only discover by some means that it is true, or that it is false—by looking at Stilpo at the time in question, for instance, to *see* whether he is then running.

Further, let us assume that it sometimes at least makes sense to speak of *asking* someone to render an R-statement true. This, of course, is only an application of the general principle that, in the case of something that someone is able to do, it sometimes makes sense to ask the person to do it. To illustrate, suppose that Crates has a bet with Metrocles that Stilpo will pass through the Diomean Gate at noon on the following day (call that day D). Now it surely seems to makes sense that Crates might ask, and perhaps even bribe, Stilpo to do just that—to pick just that time to pass through the gate—and thus render true the R-statement "Stilpo passes through the Diomean Gate at noon on day D." That a request or even a bribe would not be out of place in such circumstances suggests both that it sometimes makes sense to speak of an agent's rendering an R-statement true, and that it sometimes makes sense to ask someone—namely, the agent referred to in such a statement—to do it.

Now it is easy enough to state in general terms what one has to do in order to render a given R-statement true. One has to do *precisely* what the statement in question says one does, at precisely the time the statement says one does it. The *only* way Stilpo can render it true that he passes through the Diomean Gate at a specific time is to pass through the gate at just that time. Similarly, the *only* way he can render it false is to refrain from passing through the gate at just that time. For someone to be *able* to render an R-statement true, then, consists simply of the person's being able to do something that is *logically* both necessary and sufficient for the truth of the statement to the effect that the person does the thing in question at the time in question. Nothing else suffices, and this will need to be borne in mind.

Finally, we shall assume that, in case one speaks truly in uttering a particular R-statement at a particular time, then one also speaks truly in uttering the same R-statement at any other time. If, for example, one were to speak truly in saying that Stilpo is running at noon on a given Tuesday, one would also speak truly if one said the same thing again a week later or at any other time. This, of course, is only an application of the orthodox assumption that complete statements, or the utterances of them, are not converted from true to false, or from false to true, just by the passage of time. There are some statements, to be sure, like "Stilpo is running," that are not, as they stand, true every time they are uttered, because it is not always the case that Stilpo is running. But that is not an R-statement. If one adds to it an explicit reference to the time at which Stilpo is alleged to be running—say, at noon on a given Tuesday—then it becomes an R-statement. It also thereby becomes a statement that is true every time it is uttered, in case it is true at all, for one can on Wednesday still say truly that Stilpo was running at noon on the day preceding, in case he was, even though Stilpo may in the meantime have stopped running. This assumption, it should be noted, does not imply that *truth* and *falsity* are "properties" of "propositions" that might be gained or lost though the passage of time, nor does it imply that they are not. Some say that they are, others that they are not, and still others that such a notion is meaningless to begin with; but we, at least, prefer to take no stand on that somewhat metaphysical point.

Now let us consider three times, $t_1$, $t_2$, and $t_3$, all of them being *past*, and $t_1$ being earlier than $t_2$, which is earlier than $t_3$. Consider, then, the R-statement (S):

Stilpo walks through the Diomean Gate at $t_2$ and assume that statement, tenselessly expressed so as to avoid ambiguity in what follows, to be *true*. What we want to consider is: which, if any of the following, that are not R-statements but are statements concerning Stilpo's abilities, are also true?

1. Stilpo was at $t_3$ able to render S false.
2. Stilpo was at $t_3$ able to render S true.
3. Stilpo was at $t_1$ able to render S false.
4. Stilpo was at $t_1$ able to render S true.
5. Stilpo was at $t_2$ able to render S false.
6. Stilpo was at $t_2$ able to render S true.

## Part I: Free Will

Now the first of these is quite evidently false. If, as assumed, it is true that Stilpo was walking through the gate at $t_2$, then there is absolutely nothing he (or anyone) was able to do at $t_3$ that could render the statement false. It was, it would seem natural to say, by that time *too late* for that. He was perhaps able at $t_3$ to refrain from passing through the gate again, of course, and he was perhaps able to regret that he had walked through it, to wish he had not, and so on, but his doing any of those things would not have the least tendency to render S false. Or we might think that he was at $t_3$ able to find conclusive evidence that he had *not* walked through the gate; but that is not in fact anything that he was able to do, for he had already walked through the gate, and hence there was at $t_3$ no conclusive evidence to the contrary that he could possibly find.

The second statement seems also to be clearly false. S is, we said, true. So if anyone were, at $t_2$ (or any other time), to assert S, the individual would then be speaking truly. No sense, then, can be made of Stilpo's subsequently undertaking to *render* it true. It is in this case not just too late for him to do anything about that; it is also superfluous. What he wants to do—to render S true—he has already done.

The truth or falsity of the third statement is not quite so obvious, but it certainly appears to be false, and for the same kind of reason that (1) is false. That is, if it is true that Stilpo was walking through the gate at $t_2$, then it is difficult to see what he (or anyone) was able to do at $t_1$ that might render S false. (Analogous to the foregoing remarks, one might say, though it seems less natural to do so, that it was at that time "*too early*" for that.) Stilpo was perhaps able at $t_1$ to refrain from then and there walking through the gate, to be sure, and perhaps he did then refrain, but that does not in the least affect the truth of S, which says nothing about what he was doing at $t_1$. Or we might think that he was, at $t_1$, able to find some conclusive evidence or indication that he was not going to walk through the gate at $t_2$, but that again is not anything he was able to do; for he did walk through the gate at $t_2$, and hence there was at $t_1$ no conclusive indication to the contrary that he could possibly have found.

## Time, Truth, and Ability

To have been able at $t_1$ to render S false, Stilpo would have to have been able at $t_1$ to do something that would have been *logically* sufficient for the falsity of S. But nothing that he might have done at $t_1$ has the least logical relevance to the truth or falsity of S. We might, to be sure, suppose that he was able at $t_1$ firmly to resolve not to walk through the gate at $t_2$, but his making such a resolve would not be sufficient for the falsity of S. In fact, it has no logical relevance to S, which is, in any case, true.

Perhaps, then, Stilpo was able at $t_1$ to do something that would have been causally or physically sufficient for the falsity of S—to commit suicide, for example. Actually, this suggestion is irrelevant, for we have said that one renders an R-statement false only by doing something that is *logically* sufficient for its falsity. But even if it were relevant, it would not do. What is behind this suggestion is, obviously, that it is physically impossible that Stilpo should be walking through the gate at $t_2$ in case he killed himself at $t_1$. This is, of course, true—but if so, then it is *also* true that it was physically impossible that Stilpo should have killed himself at $t_1$ in case he was walking through the gate at $t_2$—and we have said from the start that he was then walking through the gate. The only conclusion, then, is that (3) is false, even on this enlarged and still irrelevant conception of what is involved in rendering an R-statement false.

The fourth statement appears false for reasons similar to those given for the falsity of (2). Namely, that S is true, or such that if anyone had uttered S at $t_1$, that person would have spoken truly. No sense, then, can be made of Stilpo's being able to do something at $t_1$ to *render* it true. There would have been no point, for example, in his passing through the gate at $t_1$, for that would certainly not by itself render it true that he was still passing through the gate at $t_2$. Similarly, it would not have been enough for him simply to have resolved at $t_1$ to pass through the gate at $t_2$, for that would have been entirely compatible with the falsity of S, which in any case neither says nor implies anything whatsoever about Stilpo's resolutions. People do not always act upon their resolves anyway, and there is in any case no logical necessity in their doing so. Besides,

## Part I: Free Will

anything Stilpo might do at t1 would be superfluous, even if were not pointless, for one can no more render true a statement that is true than one can render hard a piece of clay that is hard. One can only verify that it *is* true, and this, as we have seen, is something quite different. Anything Stilpo does at t1, or is able to do then, is entirely wasted.

The fifth statement likewise appears to be false. If, as we are assuming, it is true that Stilpo was passing through the gate at t2, then it is quite impossible to see what he might be able to do then and there, in addition to passing through the gate, which would, if done, render that statement false. Indeed, it is logically impossible that there should be any such supplementary action, for no matter what it was, it would have no tendency to render S false. Even if Stilpo were to declare most gravely and emphatically that he was not passing through the gate, this would not render it false that he was—it would only render him a liar. A condition logically sufficient for the truth of S—namely, Stilpo's walking through the gate—already obtains at t2 and can by no means be conjoined with another condition logically sufficient for the falsity of that statement. Now Stilpo might, to be sure, suddenly *stop* walking through the gate, which we can for now assume that he is able to do, but this would not in the least alter the truth of S. On the contrary, unless he were walking through the gate at t2, and unless, accordingly, S were true, he could not then *stop* walking. His ceasing to walk would only render it false that he was walking shortly after t2, and this is hardly inconsistent with S.

The sixth statement, finally, appears, unlike the others, to be quite evidently true in one seemingly trivial sense, but nonsensical in another. The sense in which it is true is simply this: that if S is true, then it follows that Stilpo was able to be walking through the gate at t2, that being, in fact, precisely what he was doing. It is not clear, however, what sense can be attached to his being able to render true what is true, just as it is not clear what sense could be made of someone's rendering hard some clay that is already hard.

If a piece of clay is hard, we cannot sensibly ask anyone to *render* it hard. Similarly, if Stilpo is walking through the gate, we cannot sensibly ask him to render it true that he is walking through the gate. We cannot sensibly ask him to *be* walking through the gate, for he is already doing that, and our request would be otiose and absurd, like asking a person who is sitting to be sitting, or one who is talking to be talking. We cannot ask him to *continue* walking through the gate, for that would not be to the point. It would, if done, only render it true that he was still walking through the gate at some time *after* t2, which is not what we are after. And obviously, there is nothing else we could ask him to do which is anywhere to the point.

The only conclusion we can draw is that, of the six statements before us, those that make clear sense are all false, and the only one that is true makes only trivial and dubious sense. More generally, we can say that while it might, as we assumed at the beginning, make sense to speak of being able to render an R-statement true, or being able to render such a statement false, people can in fact only render true those R-statements that are true and can only render false those that are false, and that these latter two conceptions themselves make very dubious sense.

## POSTSCRIPT (by Steven M. Cahn)

This argument is a reductio ad absurdum, assuming the truth of the opponents' position, showing its unacceptable consequences, and thereby demonstrating its falsity. In this case the opponents' position is the view widespread among philosophers that, as stated in the first sentence of the fifth paragraph, "if one speaks truly in uttering a particular R-statement at a particular time, then one also speaks truly in uttering the same R-statement at any other time." Richard Taylor and I rejected this claim, and our strategy was to introduce the plausible notion of rendering a statement true, then point out that rendering true a statement that is already true appears senseless.

Our view was that while you may speak truly in uttering an R-statement after the specified action has occurred, you do not speak truly in uttering that same R-statement before the action

## Part I: Free Will

occurs. Hence any statement that asserts or denies concerning a future action that it is going to occur, is neither true nor false, the world being as yet indeterminate with regard to the matter. In sum, logic should reflect that while the past is closed and cannot be changed, the future is open, and outcomes depend on our decisions and actions.

Incidentally, Stilpo, Crates, and Metrocles were fourth-century B.C.E. Greek philosophers; the Diomean Gate was located in Athens.

My teacher Richard Taylor was himself the author of a related controversial essay titled "Fatalism," that appeared three years before in *The Philosophical Review* and generated much discussion in the leading philosophical journals of both Britain and the United States. The highlights of that colloquy, including my first published article as well as David Foster Wallace's senior thesis in 1985 at Amherst College, which explored the issues in detail, are collected in *Fate, Time, and Language*, eds. Steven M. Cahn and Maureen Eckert (New York: Columbia University Press, 2011).

# 5

## Does God Know the Future?

IN THE BOOK OF Deuteronomy, God says to the people of Israel, "I have put before you life and death, blessing and curse. Choose life—if you and your offspring would live."[1] Did God know which option the people would choose? If so, how could their choice have been free? For if God knew they would choose life, then to have chosen death would have confuted God's knowledge—which is impossible. If God knew they would choose death, then to have chosen life would also have confuted God's knowledge. But God gave the people a genuine choice. Thus even God did not know how they would choose.

I find this line of argument persuasive, but many notable thinkers have believed it unsound. In what follows I shall present briefly a sampling of their objections and my replies.

Objection 1. "Just as your memory does not force the past to have happened, God's foreknowledge does not force the future to happen." So argued St. Augustine.[2]

Reply. My remembering that an event occurred does not cause the event's occurrence, and God's foreknowledge that an event will

---

1. *Tanakh: The Holy Scriptures* (Philadelphia: Jewish Publication Society, 1988), Dr. 30:19.

2. *On Free Choice of the Will*, trans. Thomas Williams (Indianapolis: Hackett, 1993), Book III, sec. 4, 78.

## Part I: Free Will

occur does not cause its occurrence. If I know, however, that an event occurred, then it is not now within my power to alter its occurrence. Not only won't I alter it; I can't. Similarly, if God knows that an event will occur, then it is not within God's power to alter its occurrence. Even assuming God is all-powerful, God can only do what is logically possible, for what is logically impossible is incoherent, and an incoherent task is no task at all. Thus if an event will occur, even if God does not cause its occurrence, God is bound by logic to allow its occurrence. In short, knowledge does not cause events, but, given knowledge of events, they are unavoidable.

Objection 2. "[W]e estimate the intimacy of relationship between two persons by the foreknowledge one has of the action of the other, without supposing that in either case the one or the other's freedom has thereby been endangered. So even divine foreknowledge cannot endanger freedom." Thus said the German theologian Friedrich Schleirmacher.[3]

Reply. We rarely claim more than strong belief about what others will do, for we realize that however likely our prediction, we may be proved wrong. But when we do possess knowledge, it is incompatible with free choice. For example, we know we all shall die. It follows that no one has the power to remain alive forever. If we knew not only that we would die but also when, where, and how we would die, then we could not avoid death in the known time, place, and manner. Strong beliefs can be confuted, but not knowledge.

Objection 3. "It is not true, then, that because God foreknew what would be within the power of our wills, nothing therefore lies within the power of our wills. For when He foreknew this, He did not foreknow nothing. Therefore, if He who foreknew what would lie within the power of our wills did not foreknow nothing, but something, then clearly something lies within the power of our wills even though God has foreknowledge of it." Again. St. Augustine.[4]

---

3. *The Christian Faith*, ed. H. R. Mackintosh and J. S. Stewart (Edinburgh: T. and T. Clark, 1928), 228.

4. *The City of God against the Pagans*, trans. R. W. Dyson (Cambridge: Cambridge University Press, 1998), Book V, sec. 10, 205.

## Does God Know the Future?

Reply. This line of reasoning begs the question, assuming what is supposed to be proved. If God foreknew our free choices, then they would be free. But can God foreknow our free choices? The argument I presented originally concludes that God cannot foreknow our free choices. Simply assuming the possibility of such foreknowledge carries no weight against the argument and identifies no mistake in it.

Objection 4. "[S]ince God lives in the eternal present, His knowledge transcends all movement of time and abides in the simplicity of its immediate present. It encompasses the infinite sweep of past and future, and regards all things in its simple comprehension as if they were now taking place. Thus, if you will think about the foreknowledge by which God distinguishes all things, you will rightly consider it to be not a foreknowledge of future events, but knowledge of a never changing present." So argued the Roman philosopher Boethius.[5]

Reply. We make certain choices before others. Indeed, certain choices presuppose others. For example, the choice to seek a divorce requires a prior choice to marry. Whatever is meant by the assertion that God transcends time (a murky claim), God presumably knows that we make certain choices before others. Hence God takes account of time. Admittedly, God is supposed to view the future as clearly as we view the present. Appeals to the clarity of God's knowledge, however, only underscore why that knowledge is incompatible with the freedom of choices we are yet to make.

Objection 5. [T]hough we do not know the true nature of God's knowledge . . . yet we know that . . . nothing of all existing things is hidden from Him and that His knowledge of them does not change their nature, but the possible retains its nature as a possibility. Anything in this enumeration that appears contradictory is so only owing to the structure of our knowledge, which

---

5. *The Consolation of Philosophy*, trans. Richard Green (New York: Library of Liberal Arts, 1962), Book 5, prose 6, 116.

has nothing in common with His knowledge except the name." So wrote the medieval Jewish sage Maimonides.[6]

Reply. If God's knowledge has nothing in common with human knowledge, then God's knowledge, unlike human knowledge, might not imply the truth of what is known. Thus God's knowledge, whatever its nature, may be compatible with free choice but only in some sense not relevant to the original argument. If we do not understand the meaning of the words we use, we cannot use them to make claims we understand.

Supposing that the argument with which I began can be sustained in the face of all criticism (and much more can be said on both sides), does God lack omniscience?

Not if one adopts the view, which some commentators have attributed to Aristotle,[7] that statements about future choices are neither true nor false but at present indeterminate. According to this view, it is not now true you will finish reading this entire book and not true you won't. Until you decide, the matter is indeterminate.

As the medieval Jewish philosopher Gersonides argued, to be omniscient is to know every true statement. Because it is not true you will finish reading the entire book and not true you won't, but true that the matter is indeterminate, an omniscient being does not know you will finish reading and does not know you won't, but does know the whole truth, namely, that the matter is indeterminate and depends on your free choice.

Thus assuming that God is omniscient, God knows the physical structure of the universe but not the outcome of free choices. As Gersonides wrote, "[T]he fact that God does not have the knowledge of which possible outcome will be realized does not imply any defect in God (may He be blessed). For perfect knowledge of something is the knowledge of what the thing is in reality; when

---

6. *The Guide of the Perplexed*, trans. Chaim Rabin (Indianapolis: Hackett, 1995), 163.

7. See, for example, Richard Taylor, "The Problem of Future Contingencies," *The Philosophical Review* 66 (1957), 1–28.

the thing is not apprehended as it is, this is error, not knowledge. Hence, God knows these things in the best manner possible."[8]

In other words, when God offered the people of Israel both life and death, God, although omniscient, did not know which choice they would make. God knew all that was knowable, the whole truth. But the whole truth was that the choice of life or death rested with the people of Israel. They were responsible for their decision. God awaited, but could not foresee, the outcome of their exercise of freedom.

Some may find this view unsettling, because it implies that God's knowledge, while in a sense complete, does not include within its purview definitive answers to all questions about the future. Gersonides, however, found this conclusion consistent with the Hebrew Bible. As he wrote, "God (may He be blessed), by means of the Prophets, commands men who are about to suffer evil fortune that they mend their ways so that they will avert this punishment... Now this indicates that what God knows of future events is known by Him as not necessarily occurring."[9] In short, Divine warnings imply uncertain outcomes.

Granted, certain Biblical passages may suggest, contrary to what Gersonides argued, that God knows the future in all its details, including the outcome of future free choices. Recognizing this possibility, Gersonides responded in this admirable manner, "If the literal sense of the Torah differs from reason, it is necessary to interpret these passages in accordance with the demands of reason."[10]

---

8. *The Wars of the Lord*, trans. Seymour Feldman (Philadelphia: Jewish Publication Society, 1987), vol. 2, 118.

9. Gersonides, 118.

10. Gersonides, 98.

# PART II

Religious Belief

6

## *The* Question: Plato's *Euthyphro*

To SHERLOCK HOLMES, IRENE Adler was always "the woman."[1] To philosophers, Plato's *Euthyphro* is the dialogue containing "*the* question." Although the work is one of Plato's most unified and compelling creations, its main point is so famous that references to it appear in countless philosophical contexts.

The situation in the dialogue is that Euthyphro claims to understand the nature of piety and is challenged by Socrates to define the concept. Euthyphro eventually proposes that the pious is what all the gods love. Socrates then asks the question: "Is the pious loved by the gods because it is pious, or is it pious because it is loved by the gods?" When Euthyphro replies that he does not understand, Socrates launches into an intricate argument to prove that Euthyphro's definition is unsatisfactory. While the overall import of the argument is clear, some crucial steps are compressed, making it difficult to grasp. I hope the following reconstruction of the logic involved will help clarify the argument's structure and reveal the force and elegance of the proof.

Here is the key passage, as rendered in Maureen Eckert's effective translation.[2]

---

1. Doyle, 161. The story cited is "A Scandal in Bohemia."
2. Reprinted from *Philosophical Horizons: Introductory Readings*, 2nd ed.,

## Part II: Religious Belief

*Euthyphro:* Well, I, at least, would say this is the pious, what all the gods love, and the opposite, what all the gods hate, is impious.

*Socrates:* Surely, then let us examine this again, Euthyphro, if it is well put, or should we concede and so accept our definition and those of others, and if someone should say, "it is so," then we should agree that it is so? Should one consider what the speaker means?

*Euthyphro*: One should consider this , but I certainly think, at the moment, this is well stated.

*Socrates:* Soon we'll know better, good friend. Consider this: Is the pious loved by the gods because it is pious, or is it pious because it is loved by the gods?

*Euthyphro*: I don't understand what you're saying, Socrates.

*Socrates:* I'll try to explain more clearly. We speak of something being carried and someone carrying, of something being led and someone leading, or something being seen and someone seeing—and you understand that all these are different from one another and how they are different?

*Eurthyphro*: I believe that I understand.

*Socrates:* Very well, then there is something being loved, and someone loving it is a different thing.

*Euthyphro:* How could it not be so?

*Socrates:* So, tell me then whether something that is being carried is being carried because someone carries it or for some other reason?

*Euthyphro*: No, that's it.

*Socrates*: And something being led is this way because someone leads it, and something being seen is this way because someone sees it?

*Euthyphro*: Certainly.

*Socrates:* Well, it's not that something is seen because it has the quality of being seen; but because someone sees it, the thing has this quality of being seen. Nor is something led by someone because it has the quality of being led, but because someone leads it, it has this quality of

---

eds. Steven M. Cahn and Maureen Eckert (Boston: Wadsworth, 2006), 20–31. Copyright © 2004 by Maureen Eckert and used with her permission.

## The Question: Plato's Euthyphro

being led; nor does someone carry something because it has the quality of being carried, but it has this quality of being carried because someone carries it. Well, is what I want to say clear, Euthyphro? I want to say this, if something is produced or affected, it isn't produced because it is being produced, but because it is produced, it has the quality of being produced. Nor is something affected because it's being affected. But because it is affected, it has the quality of being affected. Or do you not agree with this?

*Euthyphro:* I do.

*Socrates:* All right, then. Is what is loved something that has the quality of either being produced or being affected by someone?

*Euthyphro*: Certainly.

*Socrates*: Well, then this is like the preceding things; it's not that something is loved by those who love it because it has the quality of being loved, but it has this quality of being loved because they love it?

*Euthyphro:* Necessarily.

*Socrates:* What do we say about the pious, Euthyphro? So, it is loved by all the gods, as you say?

*Euthyphro:* Yes.

*Socrates*: Is it pious because of this, or for some other reason?

*Euthyphro:* No, because of this.

*Socrates:* All right. So, it is loved because it is pious, but it is not pious because it is loved?

*Euthyphro:* So it seems.

*Socrates:* So then, because it is loved by the gods, it has the quality of being loved and is god-loved?

*Euthyphro:* How could it not be so?

*Socrates:* The god-loved is not the pious, Euthyphro, nor is the pious god-loved, as you say it is, but one is different from the other.

*Euthyphro:* How so, Socrates?

*Socrates:* Because we agree that the pious is loved for the reason that it is pious, but it is not pious because it is loved. Is this so?

*Euthyphro:* Yes.

## Part II: Religious Belief

*Socrates:* So, something god-loved is god-loved, meaning it is loved by the gods because of this fact of its being loved, but it is not loved because it is god-loved.

*Euthyphro:* You speak the truth.

*Socrates:* So, dear Euthyphro, if the god-loved and the pious were the same thing, then the pious would be loved because it was pious, and then the god-loved would be loved because it was god-loved, if the god-loved was god-loved on account of being loved by the gods. And thus, the pious would be pious because it was loved by all the gods, yet now you see that they are opposite to one another, being completely different from each other. For one has the quality of being loved simply because it is loved, while the other is a kind of thing that is loved because it is lovable. I venture to guess, Euthyphro, that when you were asked what piety is, you did not wish to make its nature clear to me, but told me some quality it has, because the pious is affected like this, it is loved by all the gods, but you have not yet said what it is. Therefore, as a friend, do not keep this hidden, but once again from the beginning, explain what piety is.

Socrates relies throughout on a common distinction between a thing or person who is receiving love, the loved one, and a person who is giving love, the loving one. To use a more specific example than Plato offers, we can distinguish John, who is loved, from Mary, who is loving him. Mary's loving John is the reason he is loved. That he is loved is not the reason Mary is loving him; rather, she is loving him due to certain lovable characteristics he possesses. In other words, John is loved because he is *being* loved, and he is *being* loved because of his lovable nature. He is not being loved because he is loved.

Socrates illustrates this point by a series of analogies. A thing is carried because it is *being* carried; it is not *being* carried because it is carried. A thing is led because it is *being* led; it is not *being* led because it is led. A thing is seen because it is *being* seen; it is not *being* seen because it is seen. The pattern leads to the first step of the argument.

## The Question: Plato's Euthyphro

1. A thing is loved by someone because it is *being* loved; it is not *being* loved because it is loved.

2. Why is the pious *being* loved? It is not *being* loved because it is loved—that possibility is ruled out by (1); instead, it is *being* loved because it is pious (i.e., of a pious nature).

3. So, restating (2), the pious is *being* loved because it is pious; it is not pious because it is *being* loved.

4. After substituting in (1) "what is loved by all the gods " for "A thing" and "all the gods" for "someone," the result is: "What is loved by the gods is loved by all the gods because it is *being* loved; it is not *being* loved because it is loved.

5. According to Euthyphro, "the pious" is equivalent to "what is loved by all the gods."

6. But (3), (4), and (5) are an inconsistent triad; all of them cannot be true.

7. For assuming (3), the pious is *being* loved because it is pious, and (5), the pious is what is loved by all the gods, then after substituting "what is loved by all the gods" for "the pious" twice in (3), the result is "What is loved by all the gods is *being* loved because it is loved by all the gods.

8. But, according to (4), what is loved by all the gods is not *being* loved because it is loved; rather, it is loved by all the gods because it is *being* loved. So (3) and (5) together contradict (4).

9. Similarly, assuming (4), what is loved by all the gods is loved by all the gods because it is *being* loved, and (5) the pious is what is loved by all the gods, then after substituting "the pious" for "what is loved by all the gods," twice in (4), the result is: the pious is pious because it is *being* loved.

10. But, according to (3) the pious is not pious because it is *being* loved; rather, it is *being* loved because it is pious. So (4) and (5) together contradict (3).

How are these contradictions to be avoided? (3), (4), or (5) has to be abandoned. (4) is unlikely to be abandoned, because (4)

45

## Part II: Religious Belief

follows from (1), and (1) was a distinction accepted as clear from the start. To abandon (3) would be to say that the pious is *being* loved by all the gods for no reason at all, an implausible position. Thus the only recourse is to give up (5), thereby rejecting Euthyphro's definition of piety as "what is loved by all the gods."

Plato's argument is admittedly complex, but its conclusion is straightforward. God (or the gods) cannot make something right by declaring it right; on the contrary, God declares it right because it *is* right.

In short, morality is independent of theology. Those who assume otherwise should be reminded of *the* question.

# 7

# The Noes Have It

## Hume's *Dialogues concerning Natural Religion*

IN *JUMPERS*, A PLAY by the contemporary British dramatist Tom Stoppard, the central character, a professor of moral philosophy, reflects on the position of an atheist: "Well, the tide is running his way, and it is a tide which has turned only once in human history . . . There is presumably a calendar date—a *moment*—when the onus of proof passed from the atheist to the believer, when, quite suddenly, the noes had it."[1] I would propose as that moment the posthumous publication in 1779 of David Hume's *Dialogues concerning Natural Religion*.

"Natural religion" was the term used by eighteenth-century writers to refer to theological tenets provable by reason without appeal to revelation. The three participants in the *Dialogues* are distinguished by their views concerning the scope and limits of reason. Cleanthes claims he can present arguments that demonstrate the truth of traditional Christian theology. Demea is committed to that theology but does not believe empirical evidence can provide any defense for his faith. Philo doubts that reason

---

1. Tom Stoppard, *Jumpers* (New York: Grove Press, 1972), 25.

## Part II: Religious Belief

yields conclusive results in any field of inquiry and is especially critical of theological dogmatism.

What is the central theme of the book? The answer is not obvious, for the *Dialogues* is a work of fiction, an account offered by one literary character, Pamphilus, to another, Hermippus, of a discussion Pamphilus says he heard one summer day at the house of his teacher Cleanthes. As in any sophisticated drama, we are not simply told the point; we are shown it.

Some lessons, however, are obvious. The most widely used arguments for the existence of God are subjected to trenchant criticisms. In particular, the claim that the structure of the world provides clear evidence of God's handiwork, the so-called "teleological argument," is shown to lack cogency.

Hume, however, not only undermines arguments for the existence of God but also develops in detail what is perhaps the strongest argument against the existence of God, namely, the problem of evil. How can evil exist in a world created by an all-good, all-powerful God? No glib dismissal of this perplexing problem can survive a careful reading of Hume's work.

But more is going on in the *Dialogues* than an examination of arguments for and against the existence of God. Indeed, the three central characters agree that "the question is not concerning the BEING but the NATURE of God."[2] Yet how can we make sense of the view that something exists if all its attributes are unknown?

Suppose, for instance, you are asked whether you believe in the existence of a snark. You will inquire what a snark is, what characteristics it possesses. If you are told its nature is indescribable, what would be the sense of affirming or denying its existence? About what would you be talking? Anyone who believes in the existence of a snark but can say nothing about it is confused.

The same is true of anyone who believes in the existence of God but can say nothing about God's nature. Such belief is empty. Thus the initial agreement among Cleanthes, Demea, and Philo

---

2. David Hume, *Dialogues concerning Natural Religion And Other Writings*, ed. Dorothy Coleman (Cambridge: Cambridge University Press, 2007), 2:1. (The citation is by part and paragraph.)

that God exists is of no significance unless they come to some understanding of God's nature.

They cannot do so, however, for when the traditional arguments for the existence of God have been shown to afford no understanding of the Divine, and the problem of evil forces the believer to seek refuge in God's incomprehensibility, theism loses its meaning. I consider that insight to be the underlying theme of the *Dialogues*.

Hume's genius is demonstrated in the development of this motif, for by subtle and realistic interplay among his three main characters, he brings to light the surprising affinity between the skeptic and the person of faith, as well as the lack of affinity between the person of faith and the philosophical theist.

For example, at the opening of Part 2, Demea states that God's nature is "altogether incomprehensible and unknown to us."[3] Philo agrees and speaks of "the adorably mysterious and incomprehensible nature of the supreme being."[4] Cleanthes, however, recognizes that these views render theism vacuous, so he immediately launches into a statement of the teleological argument, thereby attempting to provide some understanding of the ways of God. Cleanthes's conclusion is that "the author of nature is somewhat similar to the mind of man."[5]

But when Philo criticizes Cleanthes's analogy, Demea, who is suspicious of any attempt to describe the Supreme Being, sides with Philo, arguing that "the infirmities of our nature do not permit us to reach any ideas, which in the least correspond to the ineffable sublimity of the divine attributes."[6] Cleanthes warns Demea that if he persists in maintaining that God is completely unknowable, he will rob theism of any sense, but Demea does not grasp this point, and, with Philo's encouragement, continues to defend his self-defeating position.

3. Hume, 2:1.
4. Hume, 2:4.
5. Hume, 2:5.
6. Hume, 3:13.

## Part II: Religious Belief

In part 9, after Philo has completed his ferocious attack on Cleanthes's version of the teleological argument, Demea suggests that they rely on the cosmological or first cause argument, the claim that because whatever exists is caused to exist by something else, the ultimate cause of the entire causal chain must be God.

By placing this argument in the mouth of Demea, Hume emphasizes that even the most ardent partisans of faith must have recourse to reason if they are to defend their position. Furthermore, Hume is suggesting that those who affirm the incomprehensibility of God do not quite mean what they say, because they are prepared to try to offer some description of the Divine, even if it be so abstract a one as "necessarily existent being . . . which determined something to exist rather than nothing."[7]

Demea's argument is initially undermined not by Philo but by Cleanthes, who argues that the phrase "necessary existence" has no meaning and, furthermore, that no sense can be given to the notion of a first cause that is supposed to stand apart from the entire causal chain. Cleanthes's willingness to deny significance to Demea's concept of God serves as a reminder that anyone who enters the arena of reason is subject to attack by all those committed to rationality, be they theists or atheists.

In Part 10, where the subject of discussion turns to the evils in the world, Cleanthes again finds himself opposing Philo and Demea, both of whom defend the view that "[t]he whole earth . . . is cursed and polluted."[8] Cleanthes realizes that Philo can utilize the ills of the world to discredit the existence of a God who is all-good and all-powerful, but Demea fails to appreciate this difficulty, for he is confident that present evils will be rectified at some other time and place.

Cleanthes, however, is appalled by this line of reasoning, because it amounts to nothing more than an attempt to explain away the damaging evidence of evil by appeal to an arbitrary supposition about an unknown afterlife. Cleanthes understands, as Demea does not, that taking a leap of faith in the face of strong evidence

7. Hume, 9:3.
8. Hume, 10:8.

to the contrary raises serious doubts about the meaningfulness of one's faith.

If God's love for humanity is compatible with our being forced to endure the most terrible miseries, then what exactly is the significance of the claim that God loves us? How would things be different if God didn't love us?

Cleanthes attempts to defend the goodness of the world, hoping thereby to bolster the theistic position he and Demea share. But Philo, using evidence in part originally supplied by Demea, easily overwhelms Cleanthes, and Demea finally realizes that his apparent ally through much of the discussion has all along been his most dangerous enemy.

In Part 12, after Demea has become upset and left the company, Philo tries to soothe the displeasure exhibited by his host, Cleanthes. Many commentators have found this section puzzling, because Philo proceeds to agree with Cleanthes that the universe exhibits purpose. The reader should have become aware by this point, however, that Philo's apparently theistic utterances are not all they may seem to be, and Philo soon reveals the insignificance of his admission.

In the end he adopts the view that the whole of natural religion is reducible to one proposition: "that the cause or causes of order in the universe probably bear some remote analogy to human intelligence."[9] But because the import of this statement is negated by such qualifications as "cause or causes," "probably," and "remote analogy," the claim is at bottom neither theistic nor atheistic but simply devoid of clear sense. We are left only with Philo's observation that the proposition "affords no inference that affects human life."[10] This conclusion, if accepted, sounds the death knell for traditional theology.

In the final sentence of the book we are told that "Philo's principles are more probable than Demea's, but that those of Cleanthes approach still nearer to the truth."[11] Those who assume

---

9. Hume, 12:33.
10. Hume, 12:33.
11. Hume, 12:34.

## Part II: Religious Belief

this summation to be Hume's find it perplexing, because so many of Cleanthes's arguments have been undermined throughout the work. The statement, however, is not Hume's but that of the narrator Pamphilus, who, as a student of Cleanthes, understandably finds Cleanthes's position the most persuasive of the three.

Why should Hume have ended the *Dialogues* with a misleading assessment of the discussion? A plausible answer is that eighteenth-century English society did not take kindly to attacks on traditional theological tenets. Because Hume had no desire to precipitate a scandal, he adopted the literary device of a narrator who at both the beginning and the end could assure suspicious readers that, regardless of what might appear to have happened in the *Dialogues*, theism is triumphant.

Indeed, Hume's friends were so fearful of the public's disapproval that, despite his precautions, they dissuaded him from publishing the manuscript. Fortunately, he took great pains to assure the work would not be lost, and it appeared in print three years after his death, although without any publisher's name attached.

Another factor that may have affected Hume's choice of an ending is to be found in the work that most strongly influenced Hume. Although present-day readers are apt to associate the dialogue form with Plato, the model for Hume's work was not of Greek but of Roman origin. Hume was an admirer of the orator, statesman, and philosopher Cicero, who approximately eighteen hundred years before had authored a treatise titled *De Natura Deorum (Of the Nature of the Gods)*.

The parallels between the two works are striking. *De Natura Deorum* takes the form of an imaginary conversation among Velleius the Epicurean, Balbus the Stoic, and Cotta the Skeptic. All participants agree that the subject of discussion is to be not the being but the nature of the gods. Velleius argues that, although the gods exist, our senses can provide no knowledge of the essence of the gods. Balbus, on the other hand, offers what he considers scientific proofs for the existence of the gods, including a form of the teleological argument. Cotta demonstrates both the emptiness of Velleius's position and the weaknesses of each proof Balbus offers, especially the teleological argument. Cotta ends the work by presenting in detail a compelling version of the problem of evil. Although the Skeptic clearly appears to have had the best of the discussion, in the last sentence of the book Cicero states that in his view the reasoning of Balbus the Stoic more nearly approaches the truth. Cicero was himself allied with skepticism, but he preferred to close by adopting the stance of a believer, and Hume, following Cicero, decided to have his narrator, Pamphilus, do likewise. Perhaps both authors sensed that prudence dictated moderation in their conclusions.

An intriguing, additional feature of the comparison between the two works is that the second head of the Stoic school was named Cleanthes. And the leading exponent of skepticism in Cicero's time, the teacher who most strongly influenced his philosophical development, was named Philo. Thus did Hume pay tribute to Cicero.

How important a work is the *Dialogues concerning Natural Religion*? Suffice to say that never before or since has traditional Christian theology faced a more dangerous philosophical attack. Readers of the *Dialogues* are invited to listen to the conversation and judge for themselves whether that theology can be plausibly defended in the face of such a brilliant and profound challenge.

# 8

## Philosophical Proofs and Religious Commitment

WE MIGHT SUPPOSE THAT religious believers would be vitally interested in philosophical proofs for the existence of God, that when a proof of God's existence is persuasively defended, believers would be most enthusiastic and when a proof is refuted, they would be seriously disappointed. Such, however, is not the case. Indeed, religious believers seem remarkably uninterested in the subject. They apparently consider discussion of such proofs to be an intellectual game with no relevance to religious belief or activity. As Søren Kierkegaard remarked, "Whoever therefore attempts to demonstrate the existence of God . . . [is] an excellent subject for a comedy of the higher lunacy."[1] The same essential point was made in a less flamboyant manner by Rabbi Mordecai M. Kaplan, who noted that the "immense amount of mental effort to prove the existence of God . . . was in vain, since unbelievers seldom become believers as a result of logical argument."[2]

---

1. Søren Kierkegaard, *Philosophical Fragments*, trans. David F. Swenson, (Princeton: Princeton University Press, 1936), 3.34.

2. Mordecai M. Kaplan, *The Future of the American Jew* (New York: The Macmillan Company, 1948), 171.

## Philosophical Proofs and Religious Commitment

In what follows I wish to explain why religious believers have so little interest in philosophical proofs for the existence of God, I believe this lack of concern is reasonable, and that whatever the philosophical significance of such proofs, they have little relevance to religion.

Suppose we assume, contrary to what most philosophers believe, that the three classic proofs for the existence of God, namely, the ontological, cosmological, and teleological, are all sound. Let us grant the existence of the most perfect conceivable being who designed and sustains the universe. What implications of this supposition would be relevant to our lives?

Some people would feel more secure in the knowledge that the world had been planned by an all-good being. Others would feel insecure, realizing the extent to which their existence depended on a decision of this being. In any case, most people, out of either fear or respect, would wish to act in accord with God's will.

Belief in God by itself, however, provides no hint whatsoever of which actions God wishes us to perform, or what we ought to do to please or obey God. We may affirm that God is all-good, yet have no way of knowing the highest moral standards. All we may presume is that, whatever these standards, God always acts in accordance with them. We might expect God to have implanted the correct moral standards in our minds, but this supposition is doubtful in view of the conflicts among people's intuitions. Furthermore, even if consensus prevailed, it might be only a means by which God tests us to see whether we have the courage to dissent from popular opinion.

Some would argue that if God exists, then murder is immoral, because it destroys what God with infinite wisdom created. This argument, however, fails on several grounds. First, God also created germs, viruses, and disease-carrying rats. Because God created these things, ought they not be eliminated? Second, if God arranged for us to live, God also arranged for us to die. By killing, are we assisting the work of God? Third, God provided us with the mental and physical potential to commit murder. Does God wish us to fulfill this potential?

## Part II: Religious Belief

Thus God's existence alone does not imply any particular moral precepts. We may hope our actions are in accord with God's standards, but no test is available to check whether what we do is best in God's eyes. Some seemingly good people suffer great ills, whereas some seemingly evil people achieve happiness. Perhaps in a future life these outcomes will be reversed, but we have no way of ascertaining who, if anyone, is ultimately punished and who ultimately rewarded.

Over the course of history, those who believed in God's existence typically were eager to learn God's will and tended to rely on those individuals who claimed to possess such insight. Diviners, seers, and priests were given positions of great influence. Competition among them was severe, however, for no one could be sure which oracle to believe.

In any case, prophets died, and their supposedly revelatory powers disappeared with them. For practical purposes what was needed was a permanent record of God's will. This requirement was met by the writing of holy books in which God's will was revealed to all.

But even though many such books were supposed to embody the will of God, they conflicted with one another. Which was to be accepted? Belief in the existence of God by itself yields no answer.

The only direct, unmistakable avenue to the divine will is an experience in which one senses the presence of God and apprehends which, if any, of the putative holy books is genuine. To be certain, however, that you are experiencing God's presence and apprehending God's will, the experience cannot be open to error, for only then can it provide an unshakeable foundation for religious commitment.

If one undergoes such an incorrigible experience, it guarantees which holy book is genuine and consequently which rituals, prayers, and actions God authorizes. Note, most importantly, that such an experience by itself validates the existence of God, for unless God's presence has been experienced, the message may not be true. Thus any further proof of God's existence is unnecessary.

## Philosophical Proofs and Religious Commitment

For someone who does not undergo what is believed to be a genuine experience of the divine, several possibilities remain open. The individual may accept another person's claim to have had such an experience, thereby accepting any holy book that has been revealed and also accepting the existence of God, because unless this other person has experienced the presence of God, the report could be mistaken.

Suppose, though, that you do not accept someone else's report of an experience of God. This unwillingness may be due either to philosophical doubts concerning the possibility of such an experience[3] or practical doubt that anyone has ever undergone such an experience. In either case adherence to a particular view of God's will is unreasonable.

Not surprisingly, then, religious believers show less concern than might be expected about proofs for the existence of God. If the proof is sound, it merely confirms what is already known on the stronger evidence of someone's personal experience. If the proof is unsound, it does not undermine what is already known on the basis of such experience. In either case religious experience trumps philosophical proof.

---

3. See William L. Rowe, *Philosophy of Religion: An Introduction*, Fourth Edition (Belmont, CA: Thomson/Wadsworth, 2007, 69–88.

# 9

## The Problem of Evil and the Problem of Good

FOR CENTURIES PHILOSOPHERS HAVE grappled with the problem of evil. Succinctly stated, the problem is: Could a world containing evil have been created by an omnipotent, omniscient, omni-benevolent being? Epicurus, as cited by Hume, put it most succinctly: "Is he willing to prevent evil, but not able? then is he impotent. Is he able, but not willing? then is he malevolent. Is he both able and willing? Whence then is evil?"[1]

In other words, an all-good God would do everything possible to abolish evil. An all-powerful God would be able to abolish evil. Hence if an all-good, all-powerful God existed, evil would not. But evil exists. Therefore an all-good, all-powerful God does not.

Numerous attempts have been made to provide a defense of God's goodness in the face of evil, a project known as a "theodicy," a term derived from the Greek words *theos* and *dike* meaning "God" and "justice." A promising approach, offered by John Hick,[2] begins by distinguishing two types of evil: moral and physical. Moral evils are those for which human beings are responsible, such as murder,

---

1. Hume, 10: 25.

2. John Hick, *Philosophy of Religion*, 4th ed. (Englewood Cliffs, N.J.: Prentice Hall, 1990), 39–48.

theft, and oppression. Physical evils are those for which human beings are not responsible, such as typhoons, locusts, and volcanic eruptions.

Moral evils are justified by the hypothesis that God has given us free will, the power to do good and the power to do evil. Which we do is up to us. God could have ensured that we always act rightly, but had God done so, God would have had to eliminate our free will, because a person who is forced to act rightly is not free. God is all-powerful but cannot perform an act whose description is contradictory, because such a supposed act is no act at all. For example, God cannot create a square circle, but God's inability to do so is no limitation on God's power, for by definition a circle cannot be square. Similarly, God cannot create free persons who must always act rightly, because by definition a free person is one who does not always have to do what is right. God, therefore, had to choose between creating beings who always did what was right and creating those who were free to do both right and wrong. God chose the latter, because it constituted the greater good. Thus all moral evils are justified as necessary concomitants of the best possible world God could have created, namely, a world in which people can do good freely.

Physical evils are justified by their providing the opportunity for human beings to develop moral attributes. If the world were a paradise without hardships and dangers, people would be unable to acquire the strength of character that results from standing firm in the face of difficulties. The world was intended not as a pleasure palace but as an arena of "soul-making" in which human beings grapple with their weaknesses and in so doing acquire the strength that will serve them well in some future life,

Hick defends his position further by employing what he terms the "method of negative theodicy." Suppose, contrary to fact, the world were arranged so that nothing could ever go badly. No one could harm anyone else, no one could perform a cowardly act, and no one could fail to complete any worthwhile project. Presumably, such a world could be created through innumerable acts of God, who would alter the laws of nature as necessary.

## Part II: Religious Belief

Our present ethical concepts would thereby become useless. What would fortitude mean in an environment without difficulties? What would kindness be if no one needed help? Such a world, however efficiently it promoted pleasure, would be ill-adapted for the development of the best qualities of the human personality.

Hick emphasizes that this theodicy points forward in two ways to life after death. First, although we can find many striking instances of good resulting from evil, such as dangers that produce courage or calamities that develop patience, still in many cases evils lead to selfishness or disintegration of character. Thus any divine purpose of soul-making in earthly history must continue beyond this life to achieve more than a fragmentary success.

Second, if we ask whether the business of soul-making is so worthwhile as to offset all the evils we find, the theist's answer must be in terms of a future good that is great enough to justify all that has happened.

Does this two-pronged reply to the problem succeed in blunting its force? Yes, to some extent. Those who pose the problem may claim the logical impossibility of an all-good, all-powerful God permitting the existence of evil. We have seen, however, that under certain circumstances an all-good, all-powerful God might have to allow evil to exist, for if evil were a logically necessary component of the best possible world, then God, wishing to bring about that world, would have to utilize whatever evil was necessary for the achievement of that goal. In other words, if good was impossible without evil, then evil would be required to achieve good. In that case a world containing evil might have been created by an all-good, all-powerful God.

Yet how likely is the hypothesis that we live in the best possible world and that all the evils are logically necessary for the good? Do the greatest of tragedies and horrors enhance our lives? Are we better off because of them? How plausible, after all, is Hick's theodicy? Let us test it by by considering the effectiveness of a similar approach to an analogous issue I call "the problem of good."

Suppose someone claims that the world was created by an all-powerful, all-knowing, all-evil Demon. That hypothesis comes

## The Problem of Evil and the Problem of Good

under attack from the problem of good. Succinctly stated, the problem is: Could a world containing good have been created by an omnipotent, omniscient, omni-malevolent being? To adapt the reasoning of Epicurus, "Is he willing to prevent good, but not able? then he is impotent. He is able, but not willing? then is he benevolent. Is he both able and willing? Whence then is good?"

In other words, an all-evil Demon would do everything possible to abolish good. An all-powerful Demon would be able to abolish good. Hence if an all-evil, all-powerful Demon existed, good would not. But good does exist. Therefore an all-evil, all-powerful Demon does not.

Surprisingly, we can develop a reply to the problem of good along the same lines suggested by John Hick's response to the problem of evil. We begin by distinguishing two types of goodness: moral and physical.

Moral goods are those for which human beings are responsible, acts such as altruism, generosity, and kindheartedness. Physical goods are those for which human beings are not responsible, such as sunshine, breathable air, and drinkable water.

The justification of moral goods proceeds by tying their existence to our free will. Surely, performing a bad act freely is more evil than performing it involuntarily. The Demon could have ensured that human beings would always perform bad actions, but then those actions would not have been free, because the Demon would have ensured their occurrence. Simply performing them, therefore, would not have produced the greatest possible evil, because greater evil can be produced by free persons than by unfree ones. The Demon had to provide human beings with freedom so that they might perform their bad actions voluntarily, thus maximizing evil.

As for the justification of physical goods, we should not suppose that the Demon's purpose in creating the world was to construct a chamber of tortures in which the inhabitants would be forced to endure a succession of unrelieved pains. The world can be viewed, instead, as a place of "soul-breaking," in which free human beings, by grappling with the exhausting tasks and challenges

## Part II: Religious Belief

in their environment, can thereby have their spirits broken and their wills-to-live destroyed.

This conception of the world can be supported by what, following Hick, we may call "the method of negative justification." Suppose, contrary to fact, the world were arranged so that nothing could ever go well. No one could help anyone else, no one could perform a courageous act, and no one could complete any worthwhile project. Presumably, such a world could be created through innumerable acts of the Demon, who would alter the laws of nature as necessary.

Our present ethical concepts would thereby become useless. What would frustration mean in an environment without hope? What would selfishness be if no one could use help? Such a world, however efficiently it promoted pain, would be ill-adapted for the development of the worst qualities of the human personality.

This justification, just as Hick's, points forward in two ways to life after death. First, although we can find many striking instances of evil's being produced from good, such as the pollution of beautiful lakes or the slashing of great paintings, still in many other cases good leads to altruism or strengthening of character. Therefore any demonic purpose of soul-breaking at work in earthly history must continue beyond this life to achieve more than a fragmentary success. Second, if we ask whether the business of soul-breaking is so evil that it offsets all the good we find, the answer of the demonist (that is, the analogue to a theist) must be in terms of a future evil great enough to justify all that has happened.

Does this two-pronged reply to the problem of good succeed? Yes, to some extent. Those who pose the problem may claim the logical impossibility of an all-evil, all-powerful Demon permitting the existence of good. We have seen, however, that under certain circumstances an all-evil, all-powerful Demon might have to allow good to exist, because if good were a logically necessary component of the worst possible world, then the Demon, wishing to bring about that world, would have to utilize whatever good was necessary for the achievement of that goal. In other words, if evil was impossible without good, then good would be required to

## The Problem of Evil and the Problem of Good

achieve evil. In that case a world containing good might have been created by an all-evil, all-powerful Demon.

Yet how likely is that situation? No more so than that a world containing evil might have been created by an all-good, all-powerful God.

What is the evidence that, as Hick proposes, the horrors of bubonic plague somehow contribute to a better world? What is the evidence, as the demonist suggests, that the beauty of a sunset somehow contributes to a worse world? What is the evidence, as Hick proposes, that the free will of a Stalin achieved greater good than would have been achieved by his performing right actions involuntarily? What is the evidence, as the demonist suggests, that the free will of Abraham Lincoln achieved greater evil than would have been achieved by his performing wrong actions involuntarily?

If this world is neither the worst nor the best possible, then it could not have been created by either an all-evil, all-powerful Demon or an all-good, all-powerful God. Thus although the problem of good and the problem of evil do not show either demonism or theism to be impossible, the problems show both doctrines to be highly improbable. If demonists or theists can produce any other evidence in favor of their positions, then they can increase the plausibility of their views, but otherwise the reasonable conclusion is that neither the Demon nor God exists.

# 10

## Religion without God

MOST OF US SUPPOSE that all religions are akin to the one we happen to know best, but this assumption can be misleading. For example, many Christians believe that all religions place heavy emphasis on an afterlife, although the central concern of Judaism is life in this world, not the next, Similarly, many Christians and Jews are convinced that a person who is religious must affirm the existence of a supernatural God, They are surprised to learn that religions such as Jainism, Theravada Buddhism, as well as Samkhya and Mimamsa Hinduism, deny the existence of a supreme creator of the world.

To numerous theists as well as atheists, the concept of a nontheistic religion appears contradictory. I propose to show, however, that nothing in the theory or practice of religion—not ritual, not prayer, not metaphysical belief, not moral commitment—necessitates a commitment to traditional theism. In other words, one may be religious while rejecting supernaturalism.

Consider first the concept of a ritual. It is a prescribed symbolic action. In the case of religion, the ritual is prescribed by a religious organization and the act symbolizes some aspect of religious belief. If the religion is supernaturalistic (that is, if it believes in a supernatural deity or deities), then those who reject such theology may as a result consider any ritual irrational. Yet although particular rituals may be based on irrational beliefs, nothing about the practice of ritual is inherently irrational.

Think of two people shaking hands when meeting. This act is a ritual, prescribed by our society and symbolic of the individuals' mutual respect. The act is in no way irrational. If people shook hands in order to ward off evil demons, then shaking hands would indeed be irrational. That reason, however, is not why people shake hands. The ritual may have originated as a gesture of peace indicating that the proffered hand is without a weapon. Regardless, the ritual has no connection with God or demons but now indicates the respectful attitude one person has toward another.

Some might assume that the ritual of handshaking escapes irrationality only because the ritual is not prescribed by any specific organization and is not part of an elaborate ceremony. To see that this assumption is false, consider the graduation ceremony at a college. The graduates and faculty members all wear peculiar hats and robes, and the participants stand and sit at appropriate times. The ceremony, however, is not at all irrational. Indeed, the rites of graduation day, far from being irrational, are symbolic of commitment to the process of education and the life of reason.

At first glance, rituals may seem a comparatively insignificant feature of life, yet they are a pervasive and treasured aspect of human experience. Who would want to eliminate the customs associated with holidays such as Memorial Day or Thanksgiving? What would college football be without songs, cheers, flags, and the innumerable other symbolic features surrounding the game? Those who disdain popular rituals typically proceed to establish their own distinctive ones, such as characteristic habits of dress that symbolize a rejection of traditional mores.

Religious persons, like all others, search for an appropriate means of emphasizing their commitment to a group or its values. Rituals provide such a means. Granted, supernaturalistic religion has often fused its rituals with superstition, but nonreligious rituals can be equally superstitious. For instance, most Americans view the Fourth of July as an occasion on which they can express pride

## Part II: Religious Belief

in their country's heritage. With this purpose in mind, the holiday is one of great significance. If, however, the singing of the fourth verse of "The Star-Spangled Banner" four times on the Fourth of July were thought to protect our country against future disasters, then the original meaning of the holiday would be lost in a maze of superstition.

A naturalistic (that is, non-supernaturalistic) religion need not utilize ritual in a superstitious manner, because such a religion does not employ rituals to please a benevolent deity or appease an angry one. Rather, naturalistic religion views rituals, in the words of Rabbi Jack J. Cohen as "the enhancement of life through the dramatization of great ideals."[1] If a group places great stress on justice or freedom, why should the group not utilize ritual in order to emphasize these goals? Such a use of ritual serves to solidify the group and strengthen its devotion to its expressed purposes. These are buttressed if the ritual in question has the force of tradition, having been performed by many generations who have belonged to the same group and struggled to achieve the same goals. Ritual so conceived is not a form of superstition but a reasonable means of strengthening religious commitment, as useful to naturalistic as to supernaturalistic religion.

Let us next turn to the concept of prayer. Some might suppose that naturalistic religion could have no use for prayer, because prayer is supposedly addressed to a supernatural being, and proponents of naturalistic religion do not believe in the existence of such a being. This objection, however, oversimplifies the concept of prayer, focusing attention on one type while neglecting an equally important but different sort.

Supernaturalistic religion makes extensive use of petitionary prayer, which asks a supernatural being for favors. These may range from the personal happiness of the petitioner to the general welfare of all society. Because petitionary prayer rests on the assumption that a supernatural being exists, such prayer clearly has no place in a naturalistic religion.

---

1. Jack J. Cohen, *The Case for Religious Naturalism* (1958; Eugene, OR: Wipf & Stock, 2019), 150.

## Religion without God

Not all prayers, however, are prayers of petition. Some prayers are prayers of meditation. These are not directed to any supernatural being and are not requests for granting favors. Rather, these prayers provide the opportunity for persons to rethink their fundamental commitments and rededicate themselves to their ideals. Such prayers may take the form of silent devotion or involve oral repetition of central texts. Just as Americans repeat the Pledge of Allegiance and reread the Gettysburg Address, so adherents of naturalistic religion repeat the statements of their ideals and reread the documents that embody their traditional beliefs.

Granted, supernaturalistic religions, to the extent that they utilize prayers of meditation, tend to treat these prayers irrationally by supposing that if the prayers are not uttered a precise number of times under certain specific conditions, then the prayers lose all value. Yet prayer need not be viewed in this way. Rather, as the English biologist Sir Julian Huxley wrote, prayer "permits the bringing before the mind of a world of thought which in most people must inevitably be absent during the occupation of ordinary life ... [I]t is the means by which the mind may fix itself upon this or that noble or beautiful or awe-inspiring idea, and so grow to it and come to realize it more fully."[2]

Such a use of prayer may be enhanced by song, instrumental music, and various types of symbolism. These elements fused provide the means for adherents of naturalistic religion to engage in religious services akin to those engaged in by adherents of supernaturalistic religion. The difference between the two services is that those who participate in the latter come to relate themselves to God, whereas those who participate in the former come to relate themselves to their fellow human beings and the world in which we live.

Thus far we have examined how ritual and prayer can be utilized in naturalistic religion, but to adopt a religious perspective also involves metaphysical beliefs and moral commitments. Can these be maintained without recourse to supernaturalism?

---

2. Julian Huxley, *Religion Without Revelation* (New York: New Amsterdam Library, 1957), 141.

## Part II: Religious Belief

If we use the term "metaphysics" in its usual sense, referring to the systematic study of the most basic features of existence, then a metaphysical system may be either supernaturalistic or naturalistic. Representative of a supernaturalistic theory are René Descartes and Gottfried Leibniz. Representative of a naturalistic theory are Baruch Spinoza and John Dewey.

Spinoza's *Ethics*, for example, one of the greatest of metaphysical works, explicitly rejects the view that any being exists apart from Nature itself. Spinoza identifies God with Nature as a whole and urges that the good life consists in coming to understand Nature. In his words, "our salvation, or blessedness, or freedom consists in a constant and eternal love toward God."[3] Spinoza's concept of God, however, is explicitly not supernaturalistic, and Spinoza's metaphysical system thus exemplifies not only a naturalistic metaphysics but also the possibility of reinterpreting the concept of God within a naturalistic framework.

Can those who do not believe in a supernaturalistic God commit themselves to moral principles, or is the acceptance of moral principles dependent on the acceptance of supernaturalism? Some have assumed that those who reject a supernatural God are necessarily immoral, for their denial of the existence of God leaves them free to act without fear of divine punishment. This assumption, however, is seriously mistaken.

The refutation of the view that morality must rest on belief in a supernatural God was provided more than two thousand years ago in Plato's remarkable dialogue *Euthyphro*. There Socrates asked the overconfident Euthyphro whether actions are right because God says they are right, or whether God says actions are right because they are right.

In other words, Socrates was inquiring whether actions are right because of God's fiat or whether God is subject to moral standards. If actions are right because of God's command, then anything God commands would be right. Had God commanded adultery, stealing, and murder, then adultery, stealing, and

---

3. Baruch Spinoza, *Ethics*, ed. James Gutmann (New York: Haffner, 1957), pt. 5, prop. 36, note.

murder would be right—surely an unsettling and to many an unacceptable conclusion.

Granted, some may be willing to adopt this discomforting view, but then they face another difficulty. If the good is whatever God commands, to say that God's commands are good amounts to saying that God's commands are God's commands, a mere tautology. In that case, the possibility of meaningfully praising the goodness of God would be lost.

The lesson here is that might does not make right, even if the might is the infinite might of God. To act morally is neither to act out of fear of punishment nor to act as one is commanded. Rather, it is to act as one ought to act, and how one ought to act is not dependent on anyone's power, even if the power be divine.

Thus actions are not right because God commands them; on the contrary, God commands them because they are right. What is right is independent of what God commands, for to be right, what God commands must conform to an independent standard.

We could act intentionally in accord with a moral standard without believing in the existence of God; therefore morality does not rest on that belief. Consequently those who do not believe in God can be highly moral (as well as immoral) people, and those who do believe in the existence of God can be highly immoral (as well as moral) people. This conclusion should come as no surprise to anyone who has contrasted the benevolent life of the Buddha, the inspiring teacher and atheist, with the malevolent life of the monk Tomás de Torquemada, who devised and enforced the boundless cruelties of the Spanish Inquisition.

We have now seen that naturalistic religion is a genuine possibility, because reasonable individuals may perform rituals, utter prayers, accept metaphysical beliefs, and commit themselves to moral principles without believing in supernaturalism. Indeed, even Judaism or Christianity may be reinterpreted to eliminate any commitment to supernaturalism.

Here, for example, is how Rabbi Mordecai M. Kaplan, an opponent of supernaturalism, responds to a skeptic who asked why if the Bible isn't taken literally, Jews should nevertheless observe

## Part II: Religious Belief

the Sabbath: "We observe the Sabbath not so much because of the account of its origin in Genesis, as because of the role it has come to play in the spiritual life of our People and of mankind... The Sabbath day sanctifies our life by what it contributes to making us truly human and helping us to transcend those instincts and passions that are part of our heritage from the sub-human."[4]

And here from one of the major figures in the Christian "Death of God" movement, the Anglican Bishop of Woolwich John A. T. Robinson, who denies the existence of a God "up there" or "out there," is an account of the Holy Communion: "[T]oo often ... it ceases to be the holy meal, and becomes a religious service in which we turn our backs on the common and the community and in individualistic devotion go to 'make our communion' with 'the God out there.' This is the essence of the religious perversion, when worship becomes a realm into which to withdraw from the world to 'be with God'—even if it is only in order to receive strength to go back into it. In this case the entire realm of the non-religious (in other words, 'life') is relegated to the profane."[5]

Furthermore, a naturalistic religion can also be developed without deriving it from a supernatural religion. Consider, for example, the outlook of philosopher Charles Frankel, another opponent of supernaturalism, who nevertheless believed that religion, shorn of irrationality, can make a distinctive contribution to human life, providing deliverance from vanity, triumph over meanness, and endurance in the face of tragedy. As he put it, "it seems to me not impossible that a religion could draw the genuine and passionate adherence of its members while it claimed nothing more than to be poetry in which men might participate and from which they might draw strength and light."[6]

---

4. Mordecai M. Kaplan, *Judaism Without Supernaturalism* (New York: Reconstructionist Press, 1958), 115–16.

5. John A. T. Robinson, *Honest to God* (Philadelphia: Westminster Press, 1963), 86–87.

6. Charles Frankel, *The Love of Anxiety and Other Essays* (New York: Harper & Row, 1965), 192.

## Religion without God

Such naturalistic options are philosophically respectable. Whether to choose any of them is for each person to decide.

# PART III

Morality and Society

# 11

## John Dewey at Eighty

IN LATE 1939 JOHN Dewey reached his eightieth birthday, an anniversary that occasioned tributes in newspapers and periodicals throughout the country. The American Philosophical Association named Dewey its honorary president and requested that he retain this title for the duration of his life. Also timed to coincide with the celebration was the publication of the initial volume of Paul Arthur Schilpp's *The Library of Living Philosophers*. This book provided a critical analysis and evaluation of Dewey's philosophy by such contemporaries as Bertrand Russell, George Santayana, Hans Reichenbach, and Alfred North Whitehead. Schlipp's choice of Dewey as the first honoree is justified by one of Whitehead's remarks in the volume: "We are living in the midst of the period subject to Dewey's influence."[1] Whitehead went on to stress the significance of Dewey's philosophical thought for the development of American civilization, and he classed Dewey with philosophers whom Whitehead viewed as having performed an analogous role in their own societies—Augustine, Aquinas, Descartes, and Locke.

---

1. *The Philosophy of John Dewey*, Library of Living Philosophers, ed. Paul Arthur Schilpp (New York: Tudor Publishing Co., 1951), 477.

## Part III: Morality and Society

Most remarkably, while his friends and admirers were planning ways of honoring him for a lifetime of achievements, Dewey continued to publish articles at an extraordinary rate and also produced three longer works that are among his finest writings: *Theory of Valuation, Experience and Education,* and *Freedom and Culture.*[2] Such an accomplishment at so advanced an age is astonishing and, I believe, unparalleled in the history of philosophy.

Dewey's philosophical interests were wide-ranging, including metaphysics, epistemology and philosophy of science, ethics, social and political philosophy, aesthetics, and philosophy of education. In our own day, when many admired philosophers rarely venture outside their chosen subspecialties, we should remember that most members of the philosophical pantheon assumed that their systems of thought had explanatory power in all fields of philosophical inquiry, and did not hesitate to test the adequacy of their principal ideas by applying them in one field after another. Dewey followed this tradition and thereby made significant contributions to virtually every area of philosophy.

He consistently maintained that the most reliable method of reaching the truth about any subject matter is the pattern of inquiry exemplified in science: the evaluation of hypotheses by drawing their implications and subjecting them to empirical testing under controlled conditions. In short, Dewey stressed that ideas are to be judged not by their origins but by their consequences.

The most common objection to his view comes from those who grant the scientific method's effectiveness in acquiring factual knowledge but question its usefulness in determining matters of value. Dewey explicitly replied to this familiar challenge in his *Theory of Valuation*, a monograph he contributed to *The Foundations of the Unity of Science*, a two-volume work edited by Otto Neurath, an Austrian philosopher who was a leading member of the Vienna Circle, that group of logical positivists centered in Vienna University during the 1920s and 1930s.

---

2. *The Later Works of John Dewey, 1925–1953*, vol. 13, ed. Jo Ann Boydston (Carbondale: Souther Illinois University Press, 1988).

## John Dewey at Eighty

As is evident from the monograph, Dewey had his differences with the logical positivists, but he liked Neurath personally and was persuaded by him to contribute to the project. The charming story of how Neurath succeeded in enlisting Dewey's participation was told by Ernest Nagel:

> I accompanied Neurath and Sidney Hook when they called on Dewey at his home; and Neurath was having obvious difficulty in obtaining Dewey's participation in the *Encyclopedia* venture. Dewey had one objection—there may have been others, but this is the one I recall—to Neurath's invitation. The objection was that since the Logical Positivists subscribed to the belief in atomic facts or atomic propositions, and since Dewey did not think there are such things, he could not readily contribute to the *Encyclopedia*.
>
> Now at that time Neurath spoke only broken English, and his attempts at explaining his version of Logical Positivism were not very successful. Those of us who knew Neurath will remember his elephantine sort of physique. When he realized that his efforts at explanation were getting him nowhere, he got up, raised his right hand as if he were taking an oath in a court of law (thereby almost filling Dewey's living room), and solely declaring, "I *swear* we don't believe in atomic propositions."
>
> The pronouncement won the day for Neurath. Dewey agreed to write the monograph, and ended by saying, "Well, we ought to celebrate," and brought out the liquor and mixed a drink.[3]

Thus did Dewey come to write *Theory of Valuation*.

The essence of his insightful view about the nature of moral judgments is that they are neither mere expressions of emotion nor revelations of a transcendent order but rather statements of human ideals, emerging from and testable in experience. What is desired, therefore, may not prove desirable, once consideration is

---

3. *Dialogue on John Dewey*, ed. Corliss Lamont (New York: Horizon Press, 1959), 11–12.

## Part III: Morality and Society

given to both the means need to achieve the ends, and the consequences of the ends themselves.

Dewey's stress on the continuity of means and ends has led some critics to suppose that he denied the concept of an end-in-itself. Brand Blanshard, for example, asked, "What is it that has led Dewey to this strange theory that we can attach no value to ends in themselves?"[4] Dewey, however, proposed no such theory. As he wrote in *Democracy and Education*: "All that we can be sure of educationally is that science should be taught so as to be an end in itself in the lives of students—something worthwhile on account of its own unique intrinsic contribution to the experience of life."[5] He continued on to make the general point: "Some goods are not good *for* anything; they are just goods. Any other notion leads to an absurdity. For we cannot stop asking the question about an instrumental good, one whose value lies in its being good *for* something, unless there is at some point something intrinsically good, good for itself."[6]

Dewey stressed, however, that intelligent choices need to be made among goods and that doing so depends on empirical considerations. "For example, an end suggests itself. But, when things are weighed as means toward that end, it is found that it will take too much time or too great an expenditure of energy to achieve it, or that, if it were attained, it would bring with it certain accompanying inconveniences and the promise of future troubles. It is then appraised and rejected as a 'bad' end."[7] In this way the experimental method can inform valuation.

Just as Dewey's ethical theory steered between the Scylla and Charybdis of emotivism and intuitionism, so his education theory also avoided two hazardous alternatives. Already in 1902 in *The*

---

4. Brand Blanshard, *Reason and Goodness* (London: George Allen and Unwin, 1961), 180.

5. *The Middle Works of John Dewey*, 1899–1924, ed. Jo Ann Boydston (Carbondale: Southern Illinois University Press, 1980), 9:249.

6. *Middle Works*, 9:250

7. *Later Works*, 212.

*Child and the Curriculum*, Dewey had identified the weaknesses in what he then termed "old education" and "new education."

Proponents of the former view considered the curriculum to be the keystone of the educational process. As Dewey stated their position, "Subject-matter furnishes the end, and it determines method. The child is simply the immature being who is to be matured; he is the superficial being who is to be deepened; his is the narrow experience that is to be widened. It is his to receive, to accept. His part is fulfilled when he is ductile and docile."[8] The emphasis here is on order and discipline; the teacher is supposed to command, the student to obey.

On the other hand proponents of "new education" disregarded the curriculum and focused attention exclusively on the child. Dewey characterized their outlook as follows: "Literally, we must take our stand with the child and our departure from him. It is he and not the subject-matter which determines both quality and quantity of learning... The source of whatever is dead, mechanical, and formal in schools is found precisely in the subordination of the life and experience of the child to the curriculum."[9] The emphasis here is on spontaneity and freedom. If the student is to display initiative, the teacher must not interfere in the learning process.

In short, "old education" subordinated the child to the curriculum; "new education" subordinated the curriculum to the child. "Old education" required the teacher to be active and the student to be passive. "New education" required the student to be active and the teacher to be passive.

Perhaps the most pervasive misunderstanding of Dewey's philosophy of education is the supposition that he advocated "new education." In fact, he was as opposed to "new education" as to "old education." Here is Dewey commenting on "new education":

> The child is expected to "develop" this or that fact or truth out of his own mind. He is told to think things out, or work things out for himself, without being supplied any of the environing conditions which are requisite to

---

8. *Middle Works*, 2:276.
9. *Middle Works*, 2:276-77.

start and guide thought. Nothing can be developed from nothing; nothing but the crude can be developed out of the crude—and this is what surely happens when we throw the child back upon his achieved self as a finality, and invite him to spin new truths of nature or of conduct out of that.[10]

But what precisely did Dewey propose in place of both "old education" and "new education"? In his view the teacher's responsibility is to guide the learning process so that the child's immature powers find fulfillment in that systematized outcome of human inquiry we call "the curriculum." The aim of instruction is to discover a path from the child's own experience to the maturity of human experience reflected in art, science, and industry. A teacher who disregards the child and focuses exclusively on the curriculum is like a tour guide who reaches the proper destination but has left the party far behind. A teacher who disregards the curriculum and focuses exclusively on the child is akin to the guide who remains with the party but does not lead them anywhere. Dewey insisted that we cannot afford to neglect either the child or the curriculum; sacrificing one for the other amounts to educational failure.

Proponents of "old education" and "new education" battled throughout the early decades of the twentieth century. All that changed were the labels by which their respective positions were known. In 1938 when Dewey published *Experience and Education*, a series of lectures to the honorary society Kappa Delta Phi, he no longer referred to "old education" and "new education" but instead spoke of "traditional education" and "progressive education."

The latter term requires special comment, because Dewey is himself so often identified as the leading proponent of progressive education. In fact, however, "progressive education" was a term he rarely used. He preferred to speak of education for a "progressive society," by which he meant a society that progresses, that improves from generation to generation. Dewey viewed progressive education as nothing more or less than an education that imbues individuals with intelligence, thus enabling society to better itself, to progress.

---

10. *Middle Works*, 2:282.

The term "progressive education" became a shibboleth used by those who, in Dewey's name, argued for a position identical with that previously called "new education," a position, as we have seen, Dewey opposed. In *Experience and Education*, Dewey explicitly states his opposition to progressive education, misunderstood as the rejection of pedagogical authority and the glorification of student caprice. Dewey never fell into the trap of supposing that to recognize the dignity of each student requires the teacher to abandon the role of leader of group activities. Indeed, Dewey quoted with admiration Ralph Waldo Emerson's dictum: "Respect the child, respect him to the end, but also respect yourself."[11]

Dewey made clear that the teacher is properly held responsible for what is going on in the classroom, and with responsibility goes authority. To recognize such authority, however, is not to suggest that the teacher should act in an authoritarian manner, exercising complete control over the will of students. The appropriate relationship is that of guide, not god. *Experience and Education* analyzes and illustrates the appropriate scope and limits of this guiding role.

While educational controversies of the late 1930s were remarkably similar to disputes about schooling that had occurred three decades before, the social, political, and economic situation in the United States on the eve of World War II was hardly like that of the 1900s and was soon to be subject to unprecedented changes occurring at an ever-accelerating rate. How remarkable, therefore, that when Dewey, at the age of eighty, published *Freedom and Culture*, a study of the elements of culture that contribute to the maintenance of political freedom, he did not merely propose old solutions to new problems but provided a prophetic analysis of conditions, both internal and external, that in the years to come would threaten the welfare of our democracy.

He emphasized, for instance, that the racial and religious prejudice prevalent in the United States during the 1930s corroded decency and undermined trust in human nature. At a time when discrimination against Catholic, Jews, and African Americans was

11. *Middle Works*, 9:57.

the rule rather than the exception, Dewey recognized the evil inherent in such hatred and warned of its dangerous potential for crippling the democratic way of life.

He also recognized how similar were dictatorships of the right and the left. He noted that whether a government is Fascist or Communist, it inevitably suppresses basic freedoms, persecutes dissenters, and glorifies the Leader. While others at the time were sympathetic to the policies of the Russian government, Dewey opposed every form of totalitarianism, including the Soviet version, and he insisted on the importance of open discussion, voluntary associations, and free elections.

Nor did Dewey fall prey to isolationism. After the German offensives of 1939, he strongly supported American efforts to stem the Fascist tide. He fully appreciated, as many of his contemporaries did not, the interlocking of national and international affairs. Even before the nuclear age, he wrote of how due to remote influences, "we are at the mercy of events acting upon us in unexpected, abrupt, and violent ways."[12]

One of the central themes of *Freedom and Culture* is that individuals in the modern world increasingly find themselves in the grip of immense forces they can neither control nor understand. Dewey realized that new technologies were leading to the concentration of capital in enormous corporations, the interdependence of government and industry, and perhaps most importantly, the enormous power of what we now refer to as "the media."

He provided an especially incisive description of this latter phenomenon, emphasizing how modern forms of communication can distract the public with trivia, sensationalize events, arouse confused emotions, promulgate partisan views under the guise of serving the public interest, and, in short, create what he termed "pseudo-public opinion."[13] Particularly noteworthy is Dewey's delineation of these problems years before the era of television.

What steps did he propose in the face of the weakening of the effects of individual action? He refused to subscribe to what

12. *Later Works*, 94.
13. *Later Works*, 168.

he considered the oversimplified programs of Marxism or laissez-faire capitalism but, instead, urged unwavering commitment to democratic procedures of government, the enhancement of community life, and significant steps toward the equalization of those economic conditions he viewed as essential to equal rights.

Most importantly, Dewey believed that our control over events can be greatly enhanced by the spread of the scientific attitude in our schools and reliance on it in the resolution of public problems and the creation of cultural values. He emphasized that a democratic society is especially well-suited to promote the scientific method, for both democracy and science depend on "freedom of inquiry, toleration of diverse views, freedom of communication, the distribution of what is found out to every individual as the ultimate intellectual consumer."[14]

Dewey concluded *Freedom and Culture* not by proposing a specific political platform but by calling for "collective intelligence operating in cooperative action."[15] This characteristic phrase highlights the essence of his philosophical position: a commitment to a free society, critical intelligence and the education required for their advance.

Dewey viewed philosophy of education as the most significant phase of philosophy. Charles Frankel once noted that for Dewey "all philosophy was at bottom social philosophy implicitly or explicitly."[16] I would extend this insight and suggest that for Dewey all social philosophy was at bottom philosophy of education implicitly or explicitly. As he put it, "it would be difficult to find a single important problem of general philosophic inquiry that does not come to a burning focus in matters of the determination of the proper subject matter of studies, the choice of method of teaching, and the problem of the social organization and administration of the schools."[17]

14. *Later Works*, 135.

15. *Later Works*, 188.

16. Charles Frankel, "John Dewey's Social Philosophy," in *New Studies in the Philosophy of John Dewey*, ed. Steven M Cahn (Hanover, NH: University Press of New England, 1977), 5.

17. *Later Works*, 13:260.

## Part III: Morality and Society

Other philosophers, of course, have recognized the importance of education. Kant, for example, wrote that "the greatest and most difficult problem to which man can devote himself is the problem of education."[18] But I know of only two philosophers who exemplified this principle in their philosophical work: one was Dewey, the other was Plato. He, too, found it difficult to discuss any important philosophical problem without reference to the appropriateness of various subjects of study, methods of teaching, or strategies of learning.

But while Plato's philosophy of education rested on his belief in aristocracy and the power of pure reason, Dewey's philosophy of education rested on his belief in democracy and the power of scientific method. Plato proposed a planned society, Dewey a society engaged in continuous planning. Plato considered dialectical speculation to be the means toward the attainment of truth; Dewey maintained that knowledge is only acquired through intelligent action. And whereas Plato divided the members of his ideal society into three classes, Dewey countered that what Plato had overlooked is that "each individual constitutes his own class."[19]

Suffice it to say that John Dewey is the only thinker ever to construct a philosophy of education comparable in scope and depth to that of Plato's, And the three crucial works on which I have focused exhibit Dewey's thought in all its subtlety and power, reflecting almost eighty years of experience and a lifelong commitment to rendering all experience rational.

---

18. Immanuel Kant, *Education* (Ann Arbor: University of Michigan Press, 1960), 11.

19. *Middle Works*, 9:96.

# 12

## Two Concepts of Affirmative Action

IN MARCH 1961, LESS than two months after assuming office, President John F. Kennedy issued Executive Order 10925, establishing the President's Committee on Equal Employment Opportunity. Its mission was to end discrimination in employment by the government and its contractors. The order required every federal contract to include the pledge that "The contractor will not discriminate against any employe[e] or applicant for employment because of race, creed, color, or national origin. The contractor will take affirmative action to ensure that applicants are employed, and that employe[e]s are treated during employment, without regard to their race, creed, color, or national origin."

Here, for the first time in the context of civil rights, the government called for "affirmative action." The term meant taking appropriate steps to eradicate the then widespread practices of racial, religious, and ethnic discrimination.[1] The goal, as the President stated, was "equal opportunity in employment." In other words, *procedural* affirmative action, as I shall call it, was instituted to ensure that applicants for positions would be judged without any consideration

---

1. A comprehensive history of one well-documented case of such discrimination is Dan A. Oren, *Joining the Club: A History of Jews and Yale* (New Haven and London: Yale University Press, 1985.) Prior to the end of World War II, no Jew had ever been appointed to the rank of full professor in Yale College.

## Part III: Morality and Society

of their race, religion, or national origin. These criteria were declared irrelevant. Taking them into account was forbidden.

The Civil Rights Act of 1964 restated and broadened the application of this principle. Title VI declared that "No person in the United States shall, on the ground of race, color, or national origin, be excluded from participation in, be denied the benefits of, or be subjected to discrimination under any program or activity receiving Federal financial assistance."

Before one year had passed, however, President Lyndon B. Johnson argued that fairness required more than a commitment to such procedural affirmative action. In his 1965 commencement address at Howard University, he said, "You do not take a person who for years has been hobbled by chains and liberate him, bring him up to the starting line of a race and then say, 'you're free to compete with all the others,' and still justly believe that you have been completely fair."

Several years later, President Johnson issued Executive Order 11246, stating that "It is the policy of the Government of the United States to provide equal opportunity in Federal employment for all qualified persons, to prohibit discrimination in employment because of race, creed, color or national origin, and to promote the full realization of equal employment opportunity through a positive, continuing program in each department and agency." Two years later the order was amended to prohibit discrimination on the basis of sex.

While the aim of President Johnson's order is stated in language similar to that of President Kennedy's, President Johnson abolished the Committee on Equal Employment Opportunity, transferred its responsibilities to the Secretary of Labor, and authorized the Secretary to "adopt such rules and regulations and issue such orders as he deems necessary and appropriate to achieve the purposes thereof."

Acting on this mandate, the Department of Labor in December 1971, during the administration of President Richard M. Nixon, issued Revised Order No. 4, requiring all federal contractors to develop "an acceptable affirmative action program," including

## Two Concepts of Affirmative Action

"an analysis of areas within which the contractor is deficient in the utilization of minority groups and women, and further, goals and timetables to which the contractor's good faith efforts must be directed to correct the deficiencies." Contractors were instructed to take the term "minority groups" to refer to "Negroes, American Indians, Orientals, and Spanish Surnamed Americans." (No guidance was given as to whether having only one parent, grandparent, or great-grandparent from a group would suffice to establish group membership.) The concept of "underutilization," according to the Revised Order, meant "having fewer minorities or women in a particular job classification that would be reasonably be expected by their availability." "Goals" were not to be "rigid and inflexible quotas," but "targets reasonably attainable by means of applying every good faith effort to make all aspects of the entire affirmative action program work."[2]

Such *preferential* affirmative action, as I shall call it, requires that attention be paid to the same criteria of race, sex, and ethnicity that procedural affirmative action deems irrelevant. Is such use of these criteria justifiable in employment decisions?[3]

Return to President Johnson's claim that a person hobbled by discrimination cannot in fairness be expected to be competitive.

---

2. 41 C. F. R. 60-62:12. The Order provides no suggestion as to whether a "good faith effort" implies only showing preference among equally qualified candidates (the "tie-breaking" model), preferring a strong candidate to even stronger ones (the "plus factor" model), preferring a merely qualified candidate to strongly qualified candidates (the "trumping" model), or canceling a search unless a qualified candidate of the preferred sort is available (the "quota" model).

A significant source of misunderstanding about affirmative action results from both the government's failure to clarify which type of preference is called for by a "good faith effort" and the failure on the part of those conducting searches to inform applicants which type of preference is in use. Regarding the latter issue, see my "Colleges Should Be Explicit About Who Will Be Considered for Jobs," The Chronicle of Higher Education, 35 (30),1989, reprinted in *Affirmative Action and the University: A Philosophical Inquiry*, ed. Steven M. Cahn (Philadelphia: Temple University Press, 1993), 3–4.

3. Whether their use is appropriate in a school's admission and scholarship decisions is a different issue involving other considerations, and I shall not explore that subject in this essay.

## Part III: Morality and Society

How are we to determine which specific individuals are entitled to a compensatory advantage? To decide each case on its merits would be possible, but this approach would undermine the argument for instituting preferential affirmative action on a group basis. For if some members of a group are able to compete, why not others? Thus defenders of preferential affirmative action maintain that the group, not the individual, is to be judged. If the group has suffered discrimination, then all its members are to be treated as hobbled runners.

Note, however, that while a hobbled runner, provided with a sufficient lead in a race, may cross the finish line first, giving that person an edge prevents the individual from being considered as fast a runner as others. An equally fast runner does not need an advantage to be competitive. This entire racing analogy thus encourages stereotypical thinking. For example, recall those men who played in baseball's Negro Leagues. That these athletes were barred from competing in the Major Leagues is the greatest stain on the history of the sport. While they suffered discrimination, these players were as proficient as their counterparts in the Major Leagues. They needed only to be judged by the same criteria as all others, and ensuring such equality of consideration is the essence of procedural affirmative action.

Granted, if individuals are unprepared or ill-equipped to compete, then they ought to be helped to try to achieve their goals. Such aid, however, is appropriate for all who need it, not merely for members of particular racial, sexual, or ethnic groups.

Victims of discrimination deserve compensation. Former players in the Negro Leagues ought to receive special consideration in the arrangement of pension plans and any other benefits formerly denied these athletes due to unfair treatment. The case for such compensation, however, does not imply that present African American players vying for jobs in the Major Leagues should be evaluated in any way other than their performance on the field. To assume their inability to compete is derogatory and erroneous.

Such considerations have led recent defenders of preferential affirmative action to rely less heavily on any argument that implies

## Two Concepts of Affirmative Action

the attribution of non-competitiveness to an entire population.[4] Instead, the emphasis has been placed on recognizing the benefits society is said to derive from encouraging expression of the varied experiences, outlooks, and value of members of different groups.

This approach makes a virtue of what has come to be called "diversity."[5] As a defense of preferential affirmative action, diversity has at least two advantages. First, those previously excluded are now included not as a favor to them but as a means of enriching all. Second, no one is viewed as hobbled; each competes on a par, although with varied strengths.

Notice that diversity requires preferential hiring. Those who enhance diversity are to be preferred to those who do not. Those preferred, however, are not being chosen because of their deficiency; the larger group is deficient, lacking diversity.

What does it mean to say that a group lacks diversity? Or to put the question another way, could we decide, for example, which members of a ten-person group to eliminate in order to decrease most markedly its diversity?

So stated, the question is reminiscent of a provocative puzzle in *The Tyranny of Testing*, a 1962 book by the scientist Banesh Hoffman. In this attack on the importance placed on multiple-choice tests, he quotes the following letter to the editor of the *Times* of London:

> Sir—Among the "odd one out" type of questions which my son had to answer for a school entrance examination was: "Which is the odd one out among cricket, football, billiards, and hockey?" [In England "football" refers to the game Americans call "soccer," and "hockey" here refers to "field hockey."] The letter continued: I said billiards

---

4. See, for example, Leslie Pickering Francis, "In Defense of Affirmative Action," in Cahn, especially 24–26. She raises concerns about unfairness to those individuals forced by circumstances not of their own making to bear all the costs of compensation, as well as injustices to those who have been equally victimized but are not members of specific groups.

5. The term gained currency when Justice Lewis Powell, in his pivotal opinion in the Supreme Court's 1978 Bakke decision, found "the attainment of a diverse student body" to be a goal that might justify the use of race in student admissions. An incisive analysis of that decision is Carl Cohen, *Naked Racial Preference* (Lanham, MD: Madison Books, 1995), 55–80.

## Part III: Morality and Society

because it is the only one played indoors. A colleague says football because it is the only one in which the ball is not struck by an implement. A neighbor says cricket because in all the other games the object is to put the ball into a net ... Could any of your readers put me out of my misery by stating what is the correct answer ... ?

A day later the *Times* printed the following two letters:

Sir.—"Billiards" is the obvious answer ... because it is the only one of the games listed which is not a team game.

Sir.—football is the odd one out because ... it is played with an inflated ball as compared with the solid ball used in each of the other three.

Hoffman then continued his own discussion:

When I had read these three letters it seemed to me that good cases had been made for football and billiards, and that the case for cricket was particularly clever ... At first I thought this made hockey easily the worst of the four choices and, in effect, ruled it out. But then I realized that the very fact that hockey was the only one that could be thus ruled out gave it so striking a quality of separateness as to make it an excellent answer after all—perhaps the best. Fortunately, for my piece of mind, it soon occurred to me that hockey is the only one of the four games that is played with a curved implement.

The following day the *Times* published yet another letter, this from a philosophically sophisticated thinker.

Sir.—[The author of the original letter] ... has put his finger on what has long been a matter of great amusement to me. Of the four—cricket, football, billiards, hockey—each is unique in a multitude of respects. For example, billiards is the only one played with more than one ball at once, the only one played on a green cloth and not on a field ...

It seems to me that those who have been responsible for inventing this kind of brain teaser have been ignorant of the elementary philosophical fact that every thing is at once unique and a member of a wider class.

## Two Concepts of Affirmative Action

With this sound principle in mind, return to the problem of deciding which member of a ten-person group to eliminate in order to decrease most markedly its diversity. Unless the sort of diversity is specified, the question has no rational answer.

In searches for college and university faculty members, we know what sorts of diversity are typically of present concern: race, gender, and certain ethnicities. Why should these characteristics be given special regard?

Consider, for example, other nonacademic respects in which prospective faculty appointees can differ: age, religion, nationality, regional background, economic class, social stratum, military experience, bodily appearance, physical soundness, sexual orientation, marital status, ethical standards, political commitments, and cultural values. Why should we not seek diversity of these sorts?

To some extent schools do. Many colleges and universities indicate in advertisements for faculty positions that the schools seek veterans or person with disabilities. The City University of New York requires all searches to give preference to individuals of Italian-American descent.

The crucial point is that the appeal to diversity never favors any particular candidate. Each one adds to some sort of diversity but not another. In a department of ten, one individual might be the only African American, another the only woman, another the only bachelor, another the only veteran, another the only one under thirty, another the only Catholic, another the only Republican, another the only Scandinavian, another the only socialist, and the tenth the only Southerner.

Suppose the suggestion is made that the sorts of diversity to be sought are those of groups that have suffered discrimination. This approach leads to another problem, clearly put by John Kekes:

> It is true that American blacks, Native Americans, Hispanics, and women have suffered injustice as a group. But so have homosexuals, epileptics, the urban and the rural poor, the physically ugly, those whose careers were ruined by McCarthyism, prostitutes, the obese, and so forth . . .

## Part III: Morality and Society

There have been some attempts to deny that there is an analogy between these two classes of victims. It has been said that the first were unjustly discriminated against due to racial or sexual prejudice and that this is not true of the second. This is indeed so. But why should we accept the suggestion . . . that the only form of injustice relevant to preferential treatment is that which is due to racial or sexual prejudice? Injustice occurs in many forms, and those who value justice will surely object to all of them.[6]

Kekes's reasoning is cogent. In addition another difficulty looms for the proposal to seek diversity only of groups that have suffered discrimination. For diversity is supposed to be valued not as compensation to the disadvantaged but as a means of enriching all.

Consider a department in which most of the faculty members are women. In certain fields, for example, nursing, dental hygiene, and elementary education, such departments are common. If diversity by gender is of value, then such a department, when making its next appointment, should prefer a man. Yet men as a group have not been victims of discrimination. To achieve valued sorts of diversity, the question is not which groups have been discriminated against, but which valued groups are not represented. The question thus reappears as to which sorts of diversity are to be most highly valued. I know of no compelling answer.

Seeking to justify preferential affirmative action in terms of its contribution to diversity raises another difficulty. For preferential affirmative action is commonly defended as a temporary rather than a permanent measure.[7] Preferential affirmative action to achieve diversity, however, is not temporary.

Suppose it were. Then once an institution had appointed an appropriate number of members of a particular group, preferential affirmative action would no longer be in effect. Yet the institution may later find that it has too few members of that group. Because

---

6. Cahn, 151.

7. Consider Michael Rosenfeld, *Affirmative Action and Justice: A Philosophical and Constitutional Inquiry* (New Haven and London: Yale University Press, 1991), 336: "Ironically, the sooner affirmative action is allowed to complete its mission, the sooner the need for it will altogether disappear."

## Two Concepts of Affirmative Action

lack of valuable diversity is presumably no more acceptable at one time than another, preferential affirmative action would have to be reinstated. Thereby it would in effect become a permanent policy.

Why do so many of its defenders wish it to be only transitional? They believe the policy was instituted in response to irrelevant criteria for appointment having mistakenly been treated as relevant. To adopt any policy that continues to treat essentially irrelevant criteria as relevant is to share the guilt of those who discriminated originally. Irrelevant criteria should be recognized as such and abandoned as soon as feasible.

Some defenders of preferential affirmative action argue, however, that an individual's race, gender, or ethnicity is germane to fulfilling the responsibilities of a faculty member. They believe, therefore, that preferential affirmative action should be a permanent feature of search processes, because it takes account of criteria that should be considered in every appointment.

At least three reasons have been offered to justify the claim that those of a particular race, gender, or ethnicity are well-suited to be faculty members: first, they would be especially effective teachers of any student who shares their race, gender, or ethnicity;[8] second, they would be particularly insightful researchers because of their experiencing the world from distinctive standpoints;[9] third, they would be role models, demonstrating that those of a particular race, gender, or ethnicity can be effective faculty members.[10]

Consider in turn each of these claims. As to the presumed teaching effectiveness of the individuals in question, no empirical study supports the claim.[11] But assume compelling evidence

---

8. See, for example, Francis, 31.

9. See, for example, Richard Wasserstrom, "The University and the Case for Preferential Treatment," *American Philosophical Quarterly*, 13(4), 1976, 165–70.

10. See, for example Joel J. Kupperman, "Affirmative Action: Relevant Knowledge and Relevant Ignorance," in Cahn, 181–88.

11. Consider Judith Jarvis Thomson, "Preferential Hiring," *Philosophy and Public Affairs*, 2(4), 1973, 368: "I do not think that as a student I learned any better, or any more, from the women who taught me than from the men, and I do not think that my own women students now learn any better or any more from me than they do from my male colleagues."

## Part III: Morality and Society

were presented. It would have no implications for individual cases. A person who does not share race, gender, or ethnicity with students might teach them superbly. An individual of the students' own race, gender, or ethnicity might be ineffective. Regardless of statistical correlations, what is crucial is that individuals be able to teach effectively all sorts of students, and seeking people who give evidence of satisfying this criterion is entirely consistent with procedural affirmative action. But knowing an individual's race, gender, or ethnicity does not reveal whether that person will be effective in the classroom.

Do members of a particular race, gender, or ethnicity share a distinctive intellectual perspective that enhances their scholarship? Celia Wolf-Devine has aptly described this claim as a form of "stereotyping" that is "demeaning." As she puts it, "A Hispanic who is a Republican is no less a Hispanic, and a women who is not a feminist is no less a woman."[12] Furthermore, are Hispanic men and women supposed to have the same point of view in virtue of their common ethnicity, or are they supposed to have different points of view in virtue of their different genders?

If our standpoints are thought to be determined by our race, gender, and ethnicity, why not also by the other numerous significant respects in which people differ, such as age, religion, sexual orientation, and so on? Because each of us is unique, can anyone else share my point of view?

That my own experience is my own is a tautology that does not imply the keenness of my insight into my experience. The victim of a crime may as a result embrace an outlandish theory of racism. But neither who you are nor what you experience guarantees the truth of your theories.

To be an effective researcher calls for discernment, imagination, and perseverance. These attributes are not tied to one's race, gender, ethnicity, religion, or age. African American scholars, for example, may be more inclined to study African American literature than are non-African American scholars. But some non-African American literary critics are more interested in and more

12. Cahn, 230.

knowledgeable about African American literature than are some African American literary critics. Why make decisions based on fallible racial generalizations when judgments of individual merit are obtainable and more reliable?

Perhaps the answer lies in the claim that only those of a particular race, gender, or ethnicity can serve as role models, exemplifying to members of a particular group the possibility of their success. Again, no empirical study supports the claim, but it has often been taken as self-evident that, for instance, only a woman can be a role model for a woman, only an African American for an African American, and only a Catholic for a Catholic. In other words, the crucial feature of a person is supposed to be not what the person does but who the person is.

The logic of the situation, however, is not so clear. Consider, for example, an African American woman who is a Catholic. Presumably she serves as a role model for African Americans, women, and Catholics. Does she serve as a role model for African American men, or can only an African American man serve that purpose? Does she serve as a role model for all Catholics or only for those who are African Americans? Can I serve as a role model for anyone else, because no one else shares all my characteristics? Perhaps I can serve as a role model for everyone else, because everyone else belongs to at least one group to which I belong.

Putting aside these conundrums, the critical point is suppose to be that in a field in which discrimination has been rife, a successful individual who belongs to the discriminated group demonstrates that members of the group can succeed in that field. Obviously success is possible without a role model, for the first successful individual had none. But suppose persuasive evidence were offered that a role model, while not necessary, sometimes is helpful, not only to those who belong to the group in question but also to those prone to believe that no members of the group can perform effectively within the field. Role models would then both encourage members of a group that had suffered discrimination and discourage further discrimination against the group.

To serve these aims, however, the person chosen would need to be viewed as having been selected by the same criteria as all others. If not, members of the group that has suffered discrimination as well as those prone to discriminate would be confirmed in their common view that members of the group never would have been chosen unless membership in the group had been taken into account. Those who suffered discrimination would conclude that it still exists, while those prone to discriminate would conclude that members of the group lack the necessary attributes to compete equally.

How can we ensure that a person chosen for a position has been selected by the same criteria as all others? Preferential affirmative action fails to serve the purpose, because by definition it differentiates among people on the basis of criteria other than performance. The approach that ensures merit selection is procedural affirmative action. It maximizes equal opportunity against every form of discrimination.

The policy of appointing others than the best qualified has not produced a harmonious society in which prejudice is transcended and all enjoy the benefits of self-esteem. Rather, the practice has bred doubts about the abilities of those chosen while generating resentment in those passed over.

Procedural affirmative action had barely begun before it was replaced by preferential affirmative action. The difficulties with the latter are now clear. Before deeming them necessary evils in the struggle to overcome pervasive prejudice, why not try scrupulous enforcement of procedural affirmative action? We might thereby most directly achieve that equitable society so ardently desired by every person of good will.

# 13

## Justifying Liberal Education

SOME DEFENDERS OF LIBERAL education argue that it is the study of subjects of intrinsic rather than instrumental value, learned for their own sake, not as a means to further ends. To cite one proponent of this view, liberal education is "beyond utility."[1] Those who embrace this position are likely to speak longingly of the medieval trivium and quadrivium while expressing far less concern about recent developments in the physical and social sciences. In their eyes the curriculum is a museum for the wisdom of the past, preserved so as to avoid contamination from the laboratory or the marketplace. In the words of Eva T. H. Brann, the instructor at St. John's College whom I just quoted, "Our time is not an era in which the scene of learning can teem with much newness . . . That possibility began to vanish three centuries ago . . . We are situated so as to be capable of no other novelty . . . than renovation."[2] In essence, at the time Newton was born, human creativity was exhausted.

Even those who do not share such antiquarianism may believe that the content of a liberal education is self-justifying. The

---

1. Eva T. H. Brann, *Paradoxes of Education in a Republic* (Chicago: University of Chicago Press, 1979), 62.
2. Brann, 3.

## Part III: Morality and Society

fundamental flaw in this approach, however, was exposed long ago by John Dewey. Consider this comparatively neglected passage from his *Democracy and Education*: "We cannot establish a hierarchy of values among studies. In so far as any study ... marks a characteristic enrichment of life, its worth is intrinsic."[3] Hence, "Those responsible for planning and teaching the course of study should have grounds for thinking that the studies and topics included furnish both direct increments to enriching the lives of the pupils and also materials which they can put to use in other concerns of direct interest."[4] In other words, to argue that the content of liberal education is of intrinsic value and hence self-justifying provides no defense against the counterclaim that some alternative curriculum is also of intrinsic value and therefore self-justifying.

Another common defense of liberal education appeals to such notions as self-fulfillment, self-cultivation, or self-realization. The suggestion is that these personal goals are most effectively achieved by study of the liberal arts.

This approach, though, faces serious difficulties. No matter how such terms are understood, Garry Kasparov achieved them by playing chess and Diana Taurasi by playing basketball. Yet neither of these activities is central to anyone's concept of a liberal education. On the other hand, a significant number of those who complete such an education are discontented, disaffected, or even disoriented.

A more promising defense emphasizes the usefulness of acquiring a basic understanding of our world. After all, studying the sciences, social sciences, and humanities helps us make sense of the human condition.

A difficulty with this line of argument, however, is that it fails to demonstrate why a liberal education is significant for the many who may lack the fervor to embark on a four-year quest for knowledge. Can the enormous amount of time and money that our society commits to education be justified as a glorious effort to enable millions to sip from the font of wisdom? In that case, prudence might dictate that in light of our society's limited resources, we

---

3. *Middle Works*, 9:248.
4. *Middle Works*, 9:250.

## Justifying Liberal Education

ought to provide a liberal education only to potential intellectuals, while furnishing all others with job training. Even if that policy is rejected as inconsistent with our country's commitment to equality of opportunity, the crucial issue is why a specialist needs a general education. For example, why should a future lawyer be required to study music, a future musician chemistry, or a future chemist the foundations of law?

Some proponents of liberal education respond by observing that the most useful preparation for any career is not job-training. They argue that the concept of vocational education should be broadened to include scientific, historical, and ethical questions that illuminate any occupational path.

This reply is partially effective but does not demonstrate why an individual ought to study all the essentials of a liberal education. Granted, a future musician might be well advised to study French, German, or Italian, the philosophy of art, and even that branch of physics dealing with acoustics. But why chemistry or biology? Indeed, why any subject whose connection to music is remote?

The four previous justifications mistakenly rest the case for a uniform curriculum on factors differing from person to person. I suggest, instead, that we concentrate on our commonalities, in particular, our common responsibilities as free persons in a free society. After all, each of us is not only, for example, a farmer, an electrician, or a nurse but also a citizen, and the welfare of a democracy depends in great part on the understanding and capability of its citizenry. The justification for as many persons as possible to receive a liberal education is that it provides the knowledge, skills, and values all of us need to make a success of our experiment in self-government.

What are these essentials? In addition to possessing an understanding of the democratic system itself, every member of a democracy should be able to read, write, and speak effectively so as to be able to participate fully in the free exchange of ideas that is vital to an open society. Every member of a democracy should also be able to comprehend the range of public issues, from poverty, climate change, and ideological conflict, to the dangers of nuclear

## Part III: Morality and Society

warfare and the benefits of space research. These topics cannot be intelligently discussed by those ignorant of the physical structure of the world, the forces that shape society, or the ideas and events that form the background of present crises. Thus every member of a democracy should possess substantial knowledge of physical science, social science, world history, and national history.

The study of science assumes familiarity with the fundamental concepts and techniques of mathematics, because such notions play a critical role in the physical sciences and a ever-increasing role in the social sciences. Furthermore, to know only the results of scientific and historical investigations is not sufficient; one needs also to understand the methods of inquiry that have produced these results. No amount of knowledge brings intellectual sophistication, unless one also possesses the power of critical thinking. Every member of a democracy, therefore, should be familiar with the canons of logic and scientific method.

Still another characteristic that should be common to all members of a democracy is sensitivity to aesthetic experience. An appreciation of literature, art, and music enriches the imagination, refines the sensibilities, and provides increases awareness of our world. In a society of aesthetic illiterates, not only the quality of art suffers but also the quality of life.

In connection with literature, note that significant value is derived from reading a foreign literature in its original language. Not only does great literature lose some of its richness in translation, but learning another language increases linguistic sensitivity and makes one more conscious of the unique potentialities and limitations of any particular tongue. Such study is also a most effective means of widening cultural horizons, for understanding another language is a key to understanding another culture.

Every member of a democracy should also acquire intellectual perspective, the ability to scrutinize the fundamental principles of thought and action, encompassing both what is and what ought to be. The path to such wisdom lies in the study of those subtle analyses and grand visions that comprise philosophy. No other subject affords a stronger defense against intimidation by

## Justifying Liberal Education

dogmatism while simultaneously providing a framework for the operation of intelligence.

Thus we arrive at a justification for the study of liberal education. The more who undertake it, the better, for the ignorance of some is a threat to all. If anyone complains that our democracy provides too much education for too many, they reveal their misunderstanding of a democratic society, for how can the electorate be too educated, know too much, or be too astute? Too narrow or limited an education, however, and democracy may disappear.

# PART IV
## Well-Being

14

## Happiness and Ignorance
*CO-AUTHORED WITH CHRISTINE VITRANO*

J. L. AUSTIN WARNED philosophers against the "constant obsessive repetition of the same small range of jejune 'examples.'"[1] We place in this category the familiar case illustrating so-called false happiness: a seemingly happy woman who is unaware her husband has been cheating on her. (Interestingly, the example is never that of a seemingly happy man who is unaware his wife has been cheating on him.) We find the case not only stale but unconvincing, because while happiness may be based on a false belief, happiness, if sincerely felt, is genuine.

Here, with names masked, is a true story based on events in the world of academia. Eve is an assistant professor at Euclid University. She is happy, enjoying the campus setting, amiable colleagues, and motivated students. She is especially pleased with the head of her department, a renowned scholar who is highly complimentary about her. The head asks her to serve on important committees, represent the department in college-wide activities, and lead in planning the curriculum. She is delighted to participate in these undertakings, while she continues to relish her teaching and develop her research.

---

1. J. L. Austin, *Sense and Sensibilia* (Oxford: Oxford University Press, 1962)

## Part IV: Well-Being

In her sixth year at Euclid, she is considered for tenure. She assumes all will go smoothly, especially because she has such strong support from the department head. She recognizes, though, that her scholarship presents a problem. She has spent so much time undertaking departmental and collegial responsibilities that she has published only a couple of articles. Yet she is confident of a positive outcome because her efforts have greatly benefitted the department and the university.

But matters go awry. In view of her thin publication record, the department recommends against her receiving tenure. The head does not support her, writing that although her service has been useful, she has not demonstrated strong potential as a scholar. Eventually, after all appeals have been exhausted, Eve is rejected for tenure. She is furious at her departmental head, disappointed with her colleagues, and extraordinarily unhappy.

Now the question is: Was Eve ever happy at Euclid? Richard Kraut, for one, argues that whether a person is living happily depends on whether that individual is "attaining the important things he values, or if he comes reasonably close to this high standard."[2] Because Eve was deceived, believing she was making progress toward attaining tenure when she wasn't, Kraut would claim she was not happy.

To suppose, however, that she was unhappy (or neither happy nor unhappy) is to misdescribe the situation. In fact, she was delighted with her appointment at Euclid. Granted, her outlook eventually changed, and her happiness disappeared, but her later unhappiness didn't change her earlier happiness. Future events cannot alter past ones.

Admittedly, her past happiness was based on misreading the situation, for she did not understand the trouble she faced. Had she realized, she would not have been happy and might have sought to exit from Euclid. But she hadn't the slightest interest in leaving. Why not? Because she was happy.

---

2. Richard Kraut, "Two Conceptions of Happiness," *The Philosophical Review* 88:2 (1979), 179.

## Happiness and Ignorance

Furthermore, just as her initial happiness was obvious, so was her later unhappiness. Suppose Eve had gone to the dean to complain about the tenure decision and convey how unhappy she was. Imagine the dean replying, "You're wrong. You're not unhappy. You're just confused. You think you're unhappy, but you're not." Deans have said foolish things, but this reply would top them all. For if Eve sincerely asserted she was unhappy, then she was.

The appropriate response to examples of supposedly false happiness is that sincere expressions of happiness are never false but may sometimes be based on false assumptions. In that case the happiness is not false, but the beliefs on which it is based are false. Indeed, if happiness is based on false beliefs and the individual never finds out the truth, then the person remains happy.

In fact, whatever satisfaction you may find is invariably achieved in a setting containing incomplete or misleading information. For example, you may be happy while unaware or misled about travails of your family or friends, criticisms of you that others may express only in private, lurking threats to you or your loved ones, injustices you could mitigate that may be occurring without your awareness, and physical or mental frailties that unbeknownst to you threaten your long-term well-being. If the pervasiveness of such conditions tempts you to conclude that all happiness is false happiness, you thereby rob the term "happiness" of its usefulness in distinguishing those who are content from those who are not.

Thus we can be happy even while ignorant or mistaken about aspects of our situation. After all, happiness is hard enough to achieve without requiring that the happy person be omniscient regarding all aspects of life that might affect that individual's outlook.

# 15

## Maximizing Well-Being?

IN THE FINAL PAGES of Derek Parfit's *Reason and Persons*, he asks, "What would be best for someone, or would be most in this person's interests, or would make this person's life go, for him, as well as possible?"[1] Like Parfit I take these three questions as interchangeable, but unlike him I view them not as significant but as misguided.

Consider this pair of examples taken from Steven M. Cahn and Christine Vitrano's *Happiness and Goodness*:

> Pat received a bachelor's degree from a prestigious college and a Ph.D. in philosophy from a leading university, then was awarded an academic position at a first-rate school, and eventually earned tenure there. Pat is the author of numerous books, articles, and reviews, is widely regarded as a leading scholar and teacher, and is admired by colleagues and friends for fairness and helpfulness. Pat is happily married, has two children, enjoys playing bridge and the cello, and vacations each summer in a modest house on Cape Cod. Physically and mentally healthy, Pat is in good spirits, looking forward to years of happiness.
>
> Lee, on the other hand, did not attend college. After high school Lee moved to a beach community in

---

1. Derek Parfit, *Reasons and Persons* (Oxford: Clarendon Press, 1984), 493.

## Maximizing Well-Being?

California and is devoted to sunbathing, swimming, and surfing. Having inherited wealth from deceased parents, Lee has no financial needs but, while donating generously to worthy causes, spends money freely on magnificent homes, luxury cars, designer clothes, fine dining, golfing holidays, and extensive travel. Lee has many friends and is admired for honesty and kindness. Physically and mentally healthy, Lee is in good spirits, looking forward to years of happiness.[2]

Now for Parfit's question: What would be best for Pat and Lee? I presume the answer would be different in each case, because they have few, if any, interests in common.

Suppose Pat were named President of the Eastern Division of the American Philosophical Association, became a Grand Life Master in bridge, or was invited to play the Elgar Cello Concerto with the Boston Symphony Orchestra. Which one of these accomplishments would be best for her? The question is hard to understand. Undoubtedly Pat would take pride in any of these successes, but even Pat might not know which would work out for the best. After all, any of them might prove unfortunate. Perhaps Pat might not be able to complete a satisfactory Presidential address, might suffer a devastating loss at a bridge tournament, or might have a severe memory lapse while playing the Elgar Concerto. How would these unfortunate events affect a judgment regarding what is best for Pat? And who is to judge, Pat or others?

Now consider what would be best for Lee. Would it be additional surfing challenges, an even larger home, or travel to an especially exotic location?

Granted, none of these activities is apt to appeal to Parfit, because the underlying assumption of his discussion is that lives can be judged in accord with certain criteria dear to the hearts of philosophers, including, in Parfit's words, "to have knowledge, to be engaged in rational activity, to experience mutual love, and to be aware of beauty."

2. Steven M. Cahn and Christine Vitrano, *Happiness and Goodness; Philosophical Reflections on Living Well* (New York: Columbia University Press, 2015), 4.

## Part IV: Well-Being

But why adopt these criteria? Of course, most philosophers find philosophy to be worthwhile, just as most rugby players find rugby to be worthwhile. But why is engaging in rational speculation better than engaging in athletic competition? Why is acquiring knowledge of the history of philosophy better than acquiring vast financial resources? Why is mutual love better than independence and self-esteem? Why is awareness of beauty better than awareness of the amazing variety in the animal kingdom? In sum, as Robert B. Talisse has written, "The determination among academic philosophers to support conceptions of happiness that in effect condemn most people to lives of inescapable despondency is difficult to understand."[3]

The key point is that both Pat and Lee are satisfied with their lives. As to what would be best for them, be most in their interest, or make their lives go, for them, as well as possible, I think they wouldn't even comprehend the question. Nor do I.

---

3. Robert B. Talisse, "Foreword," in Cahn and Vitrano, xiv.

# 16

## Meaningful Lives

SUSAN WOLF ASKS "WHAT is a meaningful life?" and proposes that it involves "active engagement in projects of worth."[1] But what projects or activities are worthwhile? Wolf admits that she has "neither a philosophical theory of what objective value is not a substantive theory about what has this sort of value."

She does, however, provide numerous examples of activities that are sources of meaning and ones that are not. Among those that yield meaning are moral or intellectual accomplishments, relationships with friends and relatives, aesthetic enterprises, religious practices, climbing a mountain, training for a marathon, and caring for an ailing friend. Among those that do not yield meaning are collecting rubber bands, memorizing the dictionary, making handwritten copies of *War and Peace*, riding a roller coaster, meeting a movie star, watching sitcoms, playing computer games, solving crossword puzzles, recycling, or writing checks to Oxfam and the ACLU. Controversial cases include a life single-mindedly given to corporate law, one devoted to a religious cult, and, an example she takes from David Wiggins, a pig farmer who buys more land to

---

1. Quotations and references are from Susan Wolf, "Happiness and Meaning: Two Aspects of the Good Life," *Social Philosophy and Policy* 14 (1997), 207–25.

## Part IV: Well-Being

grow more corn to feed more pigs to buy more land to grow more corn to feed more pigs.

Numerous questions jump to mind regarding the items in these categories. Why are involvements with religious practices clearly meaningful but not devotion to a religious cult? Why is caring for an ailing friend meaningful but not providing financial support for a sick stranger? Why is solving crossword puzzles not an intellectual accomplishment? Why is meeting a movie star meaningless? Does Wolf suppose that meeting a famous philosopher would be more meaningful? Why is having met David Lewis more meaningful than having met W. C. Fields?

Furthermore, why is single-minded concentration on corporate law a controversial case? Would single-minded concentration on labor law, patent law, or constitutional law also be controversial? Does single-minded concentration on epistemology escape controversy?

Collecting rubber bands is no doubt an unusual hobby, but people have devoted their lives to collecting stamps, coins, baseball memorabilia, bottles, theatrical programs, medieval works on astrology, comic books, and numerous other objects. Are some of these collections meaningful and others not?

One of my best friends, a philosopher, devoted innumerable hours to practicing and playing golf. Another friend, also a philosopher, finds golf an utter waste of time. Is one of them right and the other wrong?

Wolf suggests that "mindless, futile, never-ending tasks" are not likely to be meaningful. These criteria, however, are questionable. For instance, physical conditioning is mindless, trying to persuade all others of your solutions to philosophical problems is futile, and seeking to eliminate all diseases is never-ending. Are these activities, therefore, without meaning? Lifting heavier and heavier weights may be mindless, futile, and never-ending, but I see no reason to derogate weightlifting.

Why not allow others to pursue their own ways of life without disparaging their choices and declaring their lives meaningless? After all, others might declare meaningless a life devoted to

## Meaningful Lives

philosophical speculation that leads to writing articles that leads to others reading those articles that leads to more philosophical speculation that leads to writing more articles that leads to others reading more articles. Why is such activity more meaningful than that engaged in by Wiggins's pig farmers?

Wolf herself admits that she enjoys eating chocolate, exercising in aerobics class, and playing computer games. Why, then, does she insist on devaluing these activities?

Responding to Wolf, psychologist Jonathan Haidt presents the case of one of his students, a woman who was passionate about horses: riding them, studying their history, and making "horse friends" with others who shared her passion. He argues that this woman found meaning in life, but he recognizes that "all of her horsing around does nothing for anyone else, and it does not make the world a better place."[2] In a reply to Haidt, Wolf surprisingly agrees with this example and adds that among the activities that might bestow meaning are basketball, lawn mower racing, and, reversing herself, solving crossword puzzles.[3]

In an effort to clarify matters, let us consider Leslie, a person who cares about others, treats them with respect, and seeks to minimize their distress. Leslie does not suffer from anxiety, alienation. frustration, disappointment, or depression, and has found contentment, although whether in basketball, crossword puzzles, lawn mower racing, stockbroking, cooking, sailing, golf, gardening, hiking, or playing mahjong I shall not specify.

Would you agree that Leslie's life has meaning, i.e. that Leslie is living well? Or to reach this conclusion do you first need to know whether Leslie is an avid reader, a sharp thinker, a lover of the fine arts, a good friend to many, an active participant in political activity, a religious adherent, a parent, or something else? I don't see why.

If a person finds delights that bring no harm, such a discovery should not be denigrated but prized. For as was said wisely more

---

2. Jonathan Haidt, "Comment," in *Meaning in Life and Why It Matters*, 92–101.

3. Wolf, *Meaning in Life and Why It Matters*, 129–30.

## Part IV: Well-Being

than two thousand years ago in the Book of Ecclesiastes, "Even if a man lives many years, let him enjoy himself in all of them, remembering how many the days of darkness are going to be."[4]

---

4. Ecc. 11:8..

# 17

## How to View Death

TWO ANCIENT ARGUMENTS—ONE OF Greek origin, the other Roman—are intended to demonstrate that we should be undisturbed about death. I want to suggest that neither line of reasoning is persuasive.

In the *Letter to Menoeceus*, Epicurus argued that death should be of no concern to the living, because those who are living are not dead and those who are dead don't exist. As he put it, "death, the most terrifying of ills, is nothing to us, since so long as we exist, death is not with us; but when death comes, then we do not exist."[1]

This outlook combines one insight with two overlooked considerations. Once we are dead, we cannot be harmed, and in that sense we have no reason to fear death. Granted, the bodily remains of the dead can be destroyed; likewise the reputation of the dead can be ruined. But in neither case are the dead harmed, for they no longer exist. Say or do what you wish about the dead, they are beyond anyone's power to help or hurt. They are gone, and no one can affect them.

In that sense, Epicurus is correct to say that while we are alive, death is not present, and once death comes, *we* are not

---

1. Epicurus, "Letter to Menoeceus," in *The Stoic and Epicurean Philosophers*, ed Whitney J. Oates, trans. C. Bailey (New York: Random House, 1940), 31.

## Part IV: Well-Being

present. Yet this insight fails to take account of two ways in which death affects us.

First, death prevents our continuing to live, and living affords us the possibility of carrying out plans and finding enjoyment. All other things being equal, longer life is preferable to shorter life. Granted, once we die, we no longer exist, but that observation does not imply that whether we die should make no difference to us.

Second, we have reason to fear the death of others about whom we care. Indeed, the death of those we love or with whom we share deep friendship may be the worst moment in our lives. The death of a parent, child, sibling, spouse, or dear friend can be so devastating that life itself loses its value for us. In that respect death is an ever-present threat.

The outlook of Epicurus was defended in a well-known argument offered by Lucretius. In *On the Nature of Things* he claimed that just as we are unconcerned whether we lived at any time before we were born, so we should be equally unconcerned whether we live at any time after we die. As he said, "Look back now and consider how the bygone ages of eternity that elapsed before our birth were nothing to us. Here, then, is a mirror in which nature shows us the time to come after our death. Do you see anything fearful in it? Do you perceive anything grim? Does it not appear more peaceful than the deepest sleep?"[2]

This argument of Lucretius, however, assumes a symmetry between past and future that is unwarranted. The two are, in fact, essentially different.

Surely I could have been born earlier by a matter of minutes or hours. And few would care deeply if they had entered the world a few months or even several years sooner. But could I have lived long before my birth? I might prefer to have been a contemporary of Socrates, Shakespeare, or George Eliot, but my parents would not yet have been born. So who would I be? In any case, the past is over, it is unchangeable, and whether I was part of it cannot be affected by present choices.

---

2. Lucretius, *On the Nature of Things*, trans. Martin Ferguson Smith (Indianapolis: Hackett, 2001), 94.

## How to View Death

But how about living centuries more? The idea makes sense and appeals to many. Indeed, with medical progress I might even add hundreds of healthy years to my life, an especially attractive option if others for whom I care could do likewise.

Who would I be if I lived much longer? Answering that question does not pose a problem, because I would still be the child of my parents, and no inconsistency is involved in supposing that all our lives might extend much further than they do at present. Unlike the past, the future is not over, it is not fixed, and whether I shall be part of it can be affected by present choices.

Thus the hope for a greatly extended life is not analogous to the hope for a much earlier birth. The former makes sense, the latter does not.

I conclude that the arguments offered by Epicurus and Lucretius do not prove that our concerns about death are unfounded. Perhaps further considerations can be adduced to defend the view that our eventual oblivion should be met with nonchalance. Otherwise, unless we share some version of what the *Book of Common Prayer* describes as the "sure and certain hope of the resurrection to eternal life,"[3] we have reason to accept Bertrand Russell's view that we are all united by "the tie of a common doom," each "condemned today to lose his dearest, tomorrow himself to pass through the gates of darkness."[4] No wonder so many view death with despair.

---

3. *The Book of Common Prayer* (New York: Penguin Books, 2012), 338.
4. Bertrand Russell, *Why I Am Not a Christian* (New York: Simon and Schuster, 1957), 115–16.

# PART V

## Puzzles

# 18

## The Strange Case of John Shmarb
CO-AUTHORED WITH L. MICHAEL GRIFFEL

ONE MORNING ART FREUND opened his newspaper and was astonished to see the following headline: "FIND MANUSCRIPT OF BRAHMS'S FIFTH SYMPHONY: LOST WORK UNCOVERED IN VIENNA HOME." The accompanying story reported that a grandson of a former student of Brahms, rummaging through an old family trunk, had unearthed some dusty pages that turned out to be an original Brahms manuscript: a fifth symphony completed just prior to the composer's death in 1897. It had never been performed or published, and, in fact, Brahms seems never to have mentioned it to anyone. According to the newspaper, members of the illustrious Vienna music circle, having seen the score, enthusiastically agreed that the work was a worthy companion to its four famous predecessors.

But no one was more enthusiastic than Art, who resolved to attend the premiere of the Fifth Symphony in Vienna on May 7, the anniversary of Brahms's birth. Only with great difficulty did Art obtain a ticket, for all the most celebrated members of the music world were to attend this momentous event.

When the great day arrived, Art's expectations were realized. The music was magnificent and the audience response

## Part V: Puzzles

overwhelming. Critics wrote with impassioned, unqualified admiration for the new masterpiece. The *Times* reported:

> The four extended movements of the Symphony are each of the highest order and exemplify many of the composer's finest traits. The intense agitation and propulsion of the opening allegro appassionato, the lilting Viennese charm of the andante, the scherzo's cross-rhythms and explosive climaxes, the all'ongarese melodies of the theme and variations finale all testify to the strong Brahmsian character of the piece. But the special significance of the composition is its unusual tendencies toward a cyclical structure, most apparent in the use of the first-movement theme to link the end of the scherzo with the finale. In addition, the main theme of the second movement returns as a counterpoint to the final variation of the last movement. Interestingly, the work is marked by the use of many more nonfunctional harmonic progressions than one encounters in Brahms's other symphonies. This feature gives the work a forward-moving restlessness and enormous impact.

A story later in the week announced that the first recording of the Fifth Symphony would be released at the end of the year by the Berlin Philharmonia. When Art arrived home, he found in his mailbox publicity releases from leading American orchestras advising subscribers that performances of the new masterpiece would be scheduled immediately upon publication of the eagerly awaited score, already in progress.

Several weeks later Art was shocked by another headline: "BRAHMS'S FIFTH SYMPHONY A FAKE: MUSIC WORLD AGHAST." Incredibly, the symphony had actually been the handiwork of a young American composer, John Shmarb, who had called a press conference to announce his achievement. He explained that after obtaining authentic paper and ink of the nineteenth century, he had forged Brahms's handwriting and arranged to have the manuscript found in the old trunk. When asked why he had concocted such an elaborate hoax, young Shmarb replied:

# The Strange Case of John Shmarb

> For the last ten years, publishers, critics, and musicologists have been dismissing my work as inconsequential because they claimed all I did was copy nineteenth-century music. Well, I finally became fed up. They weren't being fair to my music. Now that the world has judged my work as it would judge the work of any nineteenth-century composer, my genius has been acknowledged. I am not imitating Brahms. I am simply composing as a contemporary of Brahms might. I find it comfortable to write in the Romantic vein and intend to continue to do so. A great work is a great work, whether composed by Brahms or by Shmarb.

Response to Shmarb's words was swift and unanimously harsh. One German critic typified the attitude of many by denouncing Shmarb as an unscrupulous fraud. "The outrage of it all! Having to waste our time on such worthless music is criminal. Shmarb has shown himself to be a musical charlatan." A leading American avant-garde composer commented: "Shmarb has always been incapable of utilizing his abilities. His output is merely derivative. Another sad case of misdirected and misused talent." Word swiftly followed that the Berlin Philharmonia had eliminated the symphony from its recording schedule, that plans to publish the work had been abandoned at considerable cost to the publisher, and that all announced performances had been canceled.

Art was greatly disheartened at these disclosures, for his cherished experience of attending the premiere of a major Brahms work had been turned into participation in a hoax. And the more he thought about the situation, the more upset he became, for he gradually realized that an even greater disappointment was that never again would he hear that symphony he had so much enjoyed. Shmarb's words ran through his mind, "A great work is a great work." He wondered why the same critics who had praised the symphony earlier now considered it worthless. For, he thought, did the great Brahms symphony suddenly become a poor work just because it was written by Shmarb in 1968? Suppose it had been written by Stravinsky in 1928 or by Bruckner in 1888? Would it be a finer composition or more enjoyable? Is it impossible to judge the merit of an anonymous composition because the composer and date are unknown? Why cannot composers be permitted to choose for themselves the style in which they wish to compose, whether that style is original in its time, typical of its time, or typical of an earlier time? Stylistic originality has been the gift of only a few composers in the history of music. Most works, indeed most of the outstanding and best-loved musical compositions, have been written in an established idiom. Stylistic originality can be a virtue, but it is not a necessity in the creation of great art. Inventiveness within a style, although more common than radical stylistic originality, is nevertheless deserving of equal consideration and is possible for any composer writing within that style at any time.

After all, certain styles, such as that of the late Romantic period, are beloved by audiences around the world. Why must they hear only old works, composed centuries ago, in those styles? Why can they not hear compositions written by contemporary composers in classic styles that have endured the test of time?

The more Art pondered the matter, the more disturbed he was by the public response to Shmarb's Symphony. He very much wanted to hear the work again and have the opportunity to confirm his judgment that it was a masterpiece. Surely, he thought, listening to the music is the only sensible way to evaluate it. What other way could be appropriate?

## POSTSCRIPT (by Steven M. Cahn)

Apart from its musical structure, what do we know of Shmarb's Symphony? Only that critics and audiences admired it greatly and, because of factors in part external to the music, thought it a composition by Brahms.

Yet, although never having heard the work, Gordon Epperson (1921-2006), the celebrated cello teacher, disparaged it as "imitative" and "derivative,"[1] while Neil Courtney (1932-2015), longtime double bassist with the Philadelphia Orchestra, called its admirers

---

1. Gordon Epperson, "The Strange Case of John Shmarb: Some Further Thoughts," *The Journal of Aesthetics and Art Criticism*, XXXIV, 1, 1975, 23-25.

# The Strange Case of John Shmarb

"sycophants" and assured us it "would never survive extended exposure to true music lovers."[2]

Both these commentators appear certain that great composers display such individuality that no piece by one could be thought to have been written by anyone else. This claim, however, has historically been proven false. Debates have raged for decades over the authenticity of various musical, artistic, and literary works sometimes attributed to one of the masters. Might we not hear a section of Mozart's C-Minor Piano Concerto and suppose it written by Beethoven? Haven't sophisticated listeners sometimes confused a scene by Rossini with one by Donizetti? Indeed, all "true music lovers" have had the experience of turning on the radio in the middle of a lovely selection and mistaking its composer.

Thus if Shmarb's Symphony was thought to have been written by Brahms, why is the piece necessarily inferior? Before making a judgment, I would want to hear the music.

---

2. Neil Courtney, " The Strange Case of John Shmarb: An Epilogue and Further Reflections," *The Journal of Aesthetics and Art Criticism*, XXXIV, 1, 1975, 27–28.

# 19

# The Divestiture Problem

SUPPOSE I HOLD ONE hundred shares of stock in a company that has embarked on a policy I consider immoral. I, therefore, wish to divest myself of those one hundred shares. For me to sell them, someone must buy them. The buyer, however, would be purchasing one hundred shares of "tainted" stock, and I would have abetted the buyer in this immoral course of action. Granted, the prospective buyer might not believe the stock "tainted," but that consideration would be irrelevant to me, because I am convinced that, knowingly or unknowingly, the buyer would be doing what is immoral. Surely I should not take any steps that would assist or encourage the buyer in such deplorable conduct. Nor should I try to release myself from a moral predicament by entangling someone else. How, then, is principled divestiture possible?

**POSTSCRIPT**

This puzzle does not attempt to prove that divestiture is invariably a mistake but only that it cannot be justified as a moral imperative. Sometimes divestiture can be defended on strategic grounds. Likewise, it can be opposed for such reasons, because by not divesting, a stockholder maintains the leverage to bring internal pressure

## The Divestiture Problem

on the company to change its policy. Either strategy may succeed or fail, depending in any particular case on a variety of factors, including the percentage of total outstanding shares held, the attitudes of the board of directors, social and economic conditions, and so on. The puzzle does not focus on such empirical considerations but on the axiom that, regardless of circumstances, the only morally proper policy is to sell "tainted" stock.

As for the suggestion that a possessor of "tainted" stock might choose to renounce ownership rather than sell, this financially fatal strategy would amount to redistribution of the value of the divestor's shares among all other stockholders. The assets of those who had not divested would thereby be increased as would presumably their moral culpability.

The essence of the situation is that your wish to sell stock is logically equivalent to your wishing someone to buy it. But, by hypothesis, you believe it wrong for anyone to buy it. Thus your wish to sell is the wish that someone else do wrong. And that desire is immoral.

## 20

## Two Lives

JOAN EARNED A DOCTORAL degree from a first-rate university and sought appointment to a tenure-track position in which she could teach and pursue her research. Unfortunately, she received no offers and was about to accept nonacademic employment when an unexpected call came inviting her for an interview at a highly attractive school. During her visit she was told by the Dean that the job was hers, subject to one condition. She was expected to teach a course each year in which numerous varsity athletes would enroll, and she would be required to award them all passing grades even if their work was in every respect unsatisfactory. Only the Dean would know of this special arrangement.

Joan rejected the position on moral grounds and continued trying to obtain a suitable opportunity in academic life. Never again, however, was she offered a faculty position, and she was forced to pursue a career path that gave her little satisfaction. Her potential as a teacher went unfulfilled, and her planned research was left undone. Throughout her life she remained embittered.

Kate also earned a doctoral degree from a first-rate university and sought appointment to a tenure-track position in which she could teach and pursue her research. She, too, received no offers and reluctantly was about to accept nonacademic appointment when an unexpected call came inviting her for an interview at the same school Joan had visited. The Dean made Kate the identical offer that had been made to Joan. After weighing the options, Kate accepted the appointment, even though she recognized that doing so would require her to act unethically.

Kate went on to a highly successful career, became a popular teacher and renowned researcher, moved to one of the nation's most prestigious universities, and enjoyed all the perquisites attendant to her membership on that school's renowned faculty. When on rare occasions, she recalled the conditions of her initial appointment, she viewed the actions she had taken as an unfortunate but necessary step on her path to a wonderful life.

In sum, Jane acted morally but lived unhappily ever after, while Kate acted immorally but lived happily ever after. Thus I leave you with this question: Which of the two was the wiser?

# Sources

1. *A New Introduction to Philosophy,* Harper & Row, 1971.
2. *Philosophy and Phenomenological Research,* XXVII, 4, 1977. Used by permission of the journal.
3. APA blog (January 24, 2019). Used by permission.
4. *Analysis* 25, 4, 1965. At the time of publication Richard Taylor (1919–2003) was Professor of Philosophy at Columbia University.
5. *Questions about God,* eds. Steven M. Cahn and David Shatz, Oxford University Press, 2002.
6. *Newsletter on Teaching Philosophy,* 4, 2, 2005. Used with permission of the American Philosophical Association.
7. *Newsletter on Teaching Philosophy,* November 1988. Used with permission of the American Philosophical Association.
8. *American Philosophical Quarterly,* 6, 2, 1969. Used with permission of the journal.
9. *Analysis,* 37, 2, 1977.
10. *A New Introduction to Philosophy.*
11. John Dewey: The Later Works, vol. 13, ed. Jo Ann Boydston, Southern Illinois University Press, 1988.
12. *Academe,* 83, 1, 1997.
13. *A New Introduction to Philosophy.*

## Sources

14. *APA blog* (November 13, 2018). Used by permission.
15. *APA blog* (September 28, 2017). Used by permission.
16. *The Meaning of Life,* 3rd ed., eds. E. M. Klemke and Steven M. Cahn, Oxford University Press, 2007.
17. *APA blog* (December 20, 2018). Used by permission.
18. *The Journal of Aesthetics and Art Criticism,* XXXIV, 1, 1975. Used by permission of The American Society for Aesthetics. At the time of publication L. Michael Griffel was Professor of Music at Hunter College and The Graduate Center of The City University of New York.
19. *Analysis* 47, 3, 1987; 49, 3, 1989; 51, 2, 1991.
20. *Newsletter on Teaching Philosophy*, 5, 2, 2006.

# Works of Steven M. Cahn

## Books Authored

*Fate, Logic, and Time*. Yale University Press, 1967; Ridgeview Publishing Company, 1982; Wipf and Stock Publishers, 2004.

*A New Introduction to Philosophy*. Harper & Row, 1971; University Press of America, 1986; Wipf and Stock Publishers, 2004.

*The Eclipse of Excellence: A Critique of American Higher Education*. Public Affairs Press, 1973; Wipf and Stock Publishers, 2004.

*Education and the Democratic Ideal*. Nelson-Hall Company, 1979; Eugene, OR: Wipf and Stock Publishers, 2004.

*Saints and Scamps: Ethics in Academia*. Rowman & Littlefield, 1986; Rev. ed., 1994; 25th anniversary edition, 2011.

*Philosophical Explorations: Freedom, God, and Goodness*. Prometheus Books, 1989.

*Puzzles & Perplexities: Collected Essays*. Rowman & Littlefield, 2002; 2nd ed. Lexington Books, 2007.

*God, Reason, and Religion*. Thomson/Wadsworth, 2006.

*From Student to Scholar: A Candid Guide to Becoming a Professor*. Columbia University Press, 2008.

*Polishing Your Prose: How to Turn First Drafts Into Finished Work* (with Victor L. Cahn). Columbia University Press, 2013.

*Happiness and Goodness: Philosophical Reflections on Living Well* (with Christine Vitrano). Columbia University Press, 2015.

*Religion Within Reason*. Columbia University Press, 2017.

*Teaching Philosophy: A Guide*. Routledge, 2018.

## Works of Steven M. Cahn

*Inside Academia: Professors, Politics, and Policies.* Rutgers University Press, 2019.
*The Road Traveled and Other Essays.* Wipf and Stock Publishers, 2019.
*Philosophical Adventures.* Broadview Press, 2020.
*A Philosopher's Journey: Essays from Six Decades.* Wipf and Stock Publishers, 2020.
*Navigating Academic Life: How the System Works.* Routledge, 2021

## Books Edited

*Philosophy of Art and Aesthetics: From Plato to Wittgenstein* (with Frank A. Tillman). Harper & Row, 1969.
*The Philosophical Foundations of Education.* Harper & Row, 1970.
*Philosophy of Religion.* Harper & Row, 1970.
*Classics of Western Philosophy.* Hackett Publishing Company, 1977; 2nd ed., 1985; 3rd ed., 1990; 4th ed., 1995; 5th ed., 1999; 6th ed., 2003; 7th ed., 2007; 8th ed., 2012.
*New Studies in the Philosophy of John Dewey.* University Press of New England, 1977.
*Scholars Who Teach: The Art of College Teaching.* Nelson-Hall Company, 1978; Wipf and Stock Publishers, 2004.
*Contemporary Philosophy of Religion* (with David Shatz). Oxford University Press, 1982.
*Reason at Work: Introductory Readings in Philosophy* (with Patricia Kitcher and George Sher). Harcourt Brace Jovanovich, 1984; 2nd ed., 1990; (also with Peter J. Markie) 3rd ed., 1995.
*Morality, Responsibility, and the University: Studies in Academic Ethics.* Temple University Press, 1990.
*Affirmative Action and the University: A Philosophical Inquiry.* Temple University Press, 1993.
*Twentieth-Century Ethical Theory* (with Joram G. Haber). Prentice Hall, 1995.
*The Affirmative Action Debate.* Routledge, 1995; 2nd ed., 2002.
*Classics of Modern Political Theory: Machiavelli to Mill.* Oxford University Press, 1997.

# Works of Steven M. Cahn

*Classic and Contemporary Readings in the Philosophy of Education.* McGraw Hill, 1997; 2nd ed., Oxford University Press, 2012.

*Ethics: History, Theory, and Contemporary Issues* (with Peter Markie). Oxford University Press, 1998; 2nd ed., 2002; 3rd ed., 2006; 4th ed., 2009; 5th ed., 2012; 6th ed., 2015; 7th ed., 2020.

*Exploring Philosophy: An Introductory Anthology.* Oxford University Press, 2000; 2nd ed., 2005; 3rd ed., 2009; 4th ed., 2012; 5th ed., 2015; 6th ed., 2018; 7th ed., 2021.

*Classics of Political and Moral Philosophy.* Oxford University Press, 2002; 2nd ed., 2012.

*Questions About God: Today's Philosophers Ponder the Divine* (with David Shatz). Oxford University Press, 2002.

*Morality and Public Policy* (with Tziporah Kasachkoff). Prentice Hall, 2003.

*Knowledge and Reality* (with Maureen Eckert and Robert Buckley). Prentice Hall, 2003.

*Philosophy for the 21st Century: A Comprehensive Reader.* Oxford University Press, 2003.

*Ten Essential Texts in the Philosophy of Religion.* Oxford University Press, 2005; 4th ed., 2021

*Political Philosophy: The Essential Texts.* Oxford University Press, 2005; 2nd ed., 2011; 3rd ed., 2015.

*Philosophical Horizons: Introductory Readings* (with Maureen Eckert). Thomson/Wadsworth, 2006; 2nd ed., 2012.

*Aesthetics: A Comprehensive Anthology* (with Aaron Meskin). Blackwell, 2008; 2nd ed. (with Stephanie Ross and Sandra Shapshay), 2020.

*Happiness: Classic and Contemporary Readings* (with Christine Vitrano). Oxford University Press, 2008.

*The Meaning of Life, 3rd Edition: A Reader* (with E. M. Klemke). Oxford University Press, 2008; 4th ed., 2018.

*Seven Masterpieces of Philosophy.* Pearson Longman, 2008.

*The Elements of Philosophy: Readings from Past and Present* (with Tamar Szabó Gendler and Susanna Siegel). Oxford University Press, 2008.

## Works of Steven M. Cahn

*Exploring Philosophy of Religion: An Introductory Anthology.* Oxford University Press, 2009; 2nd ed., 2016; 6th ed., 2022

*Exploring Ethics: An Introductory Anthology.* Oxford University Press, 2009; 2nd ed., 2011; 3rd ed., 2014; 4th ed., 2017; 5th ed., 2020.

*Philosophy of Education: The Essential Texts.* Routledge, 2009.

*Political Problems* (with Robert B. Talisse). Prentice Hall, 2011.

*Thinking About Logic: Classic Essays* (with Robert B. Talisse and Scott F. Aikin). Westview Press, 2011.

*Fate, Time, and Language: An Essay on Free Will by David Foster Wallace* (with Maureen Eckert). Columbia University Press, 2011.

*Moral Problems in Higher Education.* Temple University Press, 2011.

*Political Philosophy in the Twenty-First Century* (with Robert B. Talisse). Westview Press, 2013.

*Portraits of American Philosophy.* Rowman & Littlefield, 2013.

*Reason and Religions: Philosophy Looks at the World's Religious Beliefs.* Wadsworth/Cengage Learning, 2014.

*Freedom and the Self: Essays on the Philosophy of David Foster Wallace* (with Maureen Eckert). Columbia University Press, 2015.

*The World of Philosophy.* Oxford University Press, 2016; 2nd ed., 2019.

*Principles of Moral Philosophy: Classic and Contemporary Approaches* (with Andrew T. Forcehimes). Oxford University Press, 2017.

*Foundations of Moral Philosophy: Readings in Metaethics* (with Andrew T. Forcehimes). Oxford University Press, 2017.

*Exploring Moral Problems: An Introductory Anthology* (with Andrew T. Forcehimes). Oxford University Press, 2018.

*Philosophers in the Classroom: Essays on Teaching* (with Alexandra Bradner and Andrew Mills). Hackett Publishing Company, 2018.

*The Annotated Kant: Groundwork for the Metaphysics of Morals.* Rowman & Littlefield, 2020.

# About the Author

STEVEN M. CAHN IS Professor Emeritus of Philosophy at the City University of New York Graduate Center, where he served for nearly a decade as Provost and Vice President for Academia Affairs, then as Acting President.

He was born in Springfield, Massachusetts, in 1942, and earned his AB from Columbia College in 1963 and his PhD in philosophy from Columbia University in 1966. After performing extensively as a pianist and organist, he embarked on a professorial career that included positions at Dartmouth College, Vassar College, the University of Rochester, New York University, and the University of Vermont, where he chaired the Department of Philosophy.

He served as a program officer at the Exxon Education Foundation, as Acting Director for Humanities at The Rockefeller Foundation, and as the first Director of General Programs at the National Endowment for the Humanities. He formerly chaired the American Philosophical Association's Committee on the Teaching of Philosophy, was the Association's Delegate to the American Council of Learned Societies, and was long-time President of The John Dewey Foundation, where he initiated and brought to fruition the John Dewey Lectures, now presented at every national meeting of the American Philosophical Association.

He is the author or editor of more than sixty books. A collection of essays written in his honor, edited by two of his former doctoral students, Robert B. Talisse of Vanderbilt University and Maureen Eckert of the University of Massachusetts Dartmouth is titled *A Teacher's Life: Essays for Steven M. Cahn*.

# Index

## A

ability, 25–32
affirmative action
    compensation for victims of discrimination, 88–89
    concepts of, 85–96
    preferential—, 87–89, 92–93, 96
    procedural—, 85, 96
African Americans, discrimination against, 81–82
American Philosophical Society, 75
Amherst College, 32
Aquinas, Thomas, 75
argument, 9
Aristotle, 36
arts, appreciation of, 100
Athens, Greece, 32
atomic proposition, 77
Austin, J.L., 105
Ayer, A. J., 18

## B

Bakke decision (U.S. Supreme Court), 89n5
begging the question, 13
behavior, predicting, 7
beliefs
    control over, 8
    knowledge and—, 34
    *See also* religious belief
Berlin Philharmonia, 122–23
Bible, 37, 69
Blanshard, Brand, 78
Boethius, 35
*Book of Common Prayer*, 117
Book of Deuteronomy, 33
Book of Ecclesiastes, 114
Brahms, Johannes, 121–24
Brann, Eva T. H., 97
Bruckner, Anton, 123
Buddha, 69
Buddhism, Theravada, 64
Buridan's Ass, 20

## C

Cahn, Steven M., 32, 108, 121
*Cambridge Dictionary of Philosophy*, 22
capitalism
    laissez-faire—, 83
    new technologies and, 82
Catholicism, 81–82
*The Child and the Curriculum* (Dewey), 78–79
choice
    knowledge and—, 34
    random, 18–20
Christianity
    "Death of God" movement, 70
    emphasis on afterlife, 64
    empirical evidence, 47–53

# Index

Christianity (cont.)
    reason and—, 47–53
    supernaturalistic religion, 64
    truth of traditional theology, 47–53
Cicero, 52–53
City University of New York, 91
Civil Rights Act, 86
Cleanthes, 53
Cohen, Jack J., 66
compensation for victims of discrimination, 88–89
Courtney, Neil, 124–25
Crates, 32
culture, understanding another, 100

## D

Darrow, Clarence, 3–6, 13–14, 17
death, how to view, 115–17
"Death of God" movement, 70
democratic system, understanding, 99–100
*Democracy and Education* (Dewey), 78, 98
Demon, existence of, 62–63
*De Natura Deorum* (*Of the Nature of the Gods*; Cicero), 52–53
Descartes, René, 68, 75
desires, control over, 8
determinism and freedom, 3–17, 18
    hard determinism, 6–15, 6n4
    logical determinism, 23
    soft determinism, 6n4, 9–15
    vs. fatalism, 21–24
Dewey, John, 69, 74–84, 98
*Dialogues Concerning Natural Religion* (Hume), 47–53
dictatorship, 82
"The Dilemma of Determinism" (James), 6n4
Diomean Gate, 32

discrimination. *See* affirmative action; prejudice
diversity, 89–94
divestiture problem, 126–27

## E

Eckert, Maureen, 32, 41
Eddington, Arthur, 9–10
education
    importance of, 78–84
    justifying liberal education, 97–101
    new vs. old, 79–81
    philosophy of, 83
    progressive, 80–81
    theory, 78–81
    traditional, 80
    vocational, 99
Emerson, Ralph Waldo, 81
employment, discrimination in, 85. *See also* affirmative action
*Encyclopedia of Ethics*, 23–24
ends. *See* means and ends
environmental factors, 4, 7, 8–9, 11
Epicurus, 58, 115–16, 117
Epperson, Gordon, 124
equal employment opportunity, 85, 86. *See also* affirmative action
equal rights, 83
*Ethics* (Spinoza), 68
ethnic discrimination, 85. *See also* affirmative action
*Euthyphro* (Plato), 41–46, 68
evil
    moral evil, 58–59
    natural evil, 58–69
    problem of, 48–53, 58–63
    racial and religious prejudice, 81–82
*Experience and Education* (Dewey), 76, 80–81

# Index

## F

false
    assumptions, 107
    future statement, 31–32, 36
    happiness (*see* happiness and ignorance)
    R-statement, 25–32
falsity. *See* false
fatalism, 21–24
"Fatalism" (Taylor), 32
*Fate, Time and Language* (Cahn and Eckert, eds.), 32
Fischer, John Martin, 23–24
*The Foundations of the Unity of Science* (Neurath, ed.), 76
Frankel, Charles, 70, 83
Franks, Bobby, 3
free action, 5, 10, 15–16. *See also* free will
free agent, 17
freedom
    defined, 10–11
    determinism and—. *See* free will
    divine foreknowledge and—, 34
*Freedom and Culture* (Dewey), 76, 81–83
free will
    determinism and freedom, 3–17
    divine foreknowledge, 33–37
    fatalism, 21–24
    moral evil/goodness, 58–63
    random choices, 18–20
    time, truth, ability, 25–32
Freund, Art, 121–24
future action/events
    determinism and—, 22–24
    divine foreknowledge, 23, 33–37
    past, symmetry between—, 116–17
    true/false statement, 31–32, 36

## G

Genesis, 70
Gersonides, 36, 37
God
    act of—, 20
    all-powerful God, 58–63
    divine foreknowledge, 23, 33–37
    divine will, 54–57
    fatalism and—, 24
    identified with Nature, 68
    omniscient, 36–37
    philosophical proofs and religious commitment, 54–57
    proving existence, 48–53, 54–57
    religion without God, 64–71
    right, declaring vs. making, 46
    time, account of, 35
good, problem of, 58–63
good faith effort, 87, 87n2
goodness
    moral, 61
    physical, 61–62
Griffel, L. Michael, 121

## H

Haidt, Jonathan, 113
*Happiness and Goodness* (Cahn and Vitrano), 108–9
happiness and ignorance, 105–7
hard determinism. *See* determinism and freedom
Hebrew Bible, 37
hereditary factors, 3–4, 7, 8–9, 11
Hick, John, 58–63
Hinduism
    Mimamsa, 64
    Samkhya, 64
Hoffman, Banesh, 89–90
Holy Communion, 70
Hook, Sidney, 77
Hospers, John, 8

# Index

Howard University, 86
Hume, David, 9, 47–53, 58
Huxley, Julian, 67

## I

"idle argument," 22, 23
ignorance and happiness, 105–7
intellectual perspective, 100–101
isolationism, 82

## J

Jainism, 64
James, William, 6n4
Johnson, Lyndon B., 86, 87
Judaism
    discrimination against, 81–82, 85n1
    emphasis on present life, 64
    supernaturalistic religion, 64
*Jumpers* (Stoppard), 47

## K

Kant, Immanuel, 84
Kaplan, Mordecai M., 54, 69–70
Kasparov, Garry, 98
Kekes, John, 91–92
Kennedy, John F., 85
Kierkegaard, Søren, 54
knowledge
    free choice and—, 34, 36
    God's vs. human's, 36
Kraut, Richard, 106

## L

laissez-faire capitalism, 83
language, understanding another, 100
La Rochefoucauld, Duc de, 7

Leibniz, Gottfried, 68
Leopold, Nathan, 3–5, 8, 13, 17
*Letter to Menoeceus* (Epicurus), 115–16
liberal education. *See* education
libertarianism, 13–16
*the Library of Living Philosophers* (Schilipp), 75
lives
    meaningful, 111–14
    two lives puzzle, 128–29
Locke, John, 75
Loeb, Richard, 3–5, 8, 13, 17
logical determinism. *See* determinism and freedom
logical positivist, 76–77
Lucretius, 116, 117

## M

Maimonides, 36
Marxism, 83
means and ends, 78
media, power of, 82
metaphysical belief, 68
Metrocles, 32
Mill, John Stuart, 9
Mimamsa Hinduism, 64
minority group, use of term, 87
miracle, 20
moral commitment, 68–71
moral evil, 58–59
moral goodness, 61
morality, independent of theology, 46
morality and society
    affirmative action, concepts of, 85–96
    John Dewey, 75–84
    liberal education, justifying, 97–101
moral judgment, essence of, 77–78
moral responsibility, 12, 16–17, 18
motive, 14–15

# Index

## N

Nagel, Ernest, 77
natural evil, 58–69
naturalistic religion, 66–71
natural religion, 47–53, 69–71
nature, God identified with, 68
"negative theodicy, method of," 59
Neurath, Otto, 76–77
Nixon, Richard M., 86
Nowell-Smith, P. H., 20

## O

*On the Nature of Things* (Lucretius), 116
order, cause(s) of, 51
Oren, Dan A., 85n1
*The Oxford Companion to Philosophy*, 22
*The Oxford Dictionary of Philosophy*, 21

## P

the paradigm-case argument, 9–13
Parfit, Derek, 108–9
past, symmetry between future, 116–17
petitionary prayer, 66
Philadelphia Orchestra, 124
Philo, 53
philosophical proofs and religious commitment, 54–57
*The Philosophical Review*, 32
physical evil, 58–59
physical goodness, 61–62
piety, nature of, 41
Plato, 41–46, 52, 68, 84
Powell, Lewis, 89n5
prayer, concept of, 66–67
   petitionary prayer, 66
   prayer of meditation, 67

prayer of meditation, 67
predestination, 23
preferential affirmative action. *See* affirmative action
prejudice, 81–82
present and knowledge, 35
President's Committee on Equal Employment Opportunity, 85
procedural affirmative action. *See* affirmative action
progressive education. *See* education
proposition, properties of, 27
pseudo-public opinion, 82
puzzles
   divestiture problem, 126–27
   Shmarb, case of John, 121–25
   two lives, 128–29

## Q

quantum mechanics, 8, 8n7
"*the* question," 41–46

## R

racial discrimination, 81–82, 85. *See also* affirmative action
random choice. *See* choice, random
reason, power of pure, 84
*Reason and Persons* (Parfit), 108
Reichenbach, Hans, 75
religion, natural, 47
religious belief
   atheist vs. believer, 47–53
   Hume's *Dialogues concerning Natural Religion*, 47–53
   philosophical proofs and religious commitment, 54–57
   Plato's *Euthyphro*, 41–46
   problem of good/evil, 58–63
   "the question," 41–46

# Index

religious belief (cont.)
    religion without God, 64–71
    traditional theism, 64
religious commitment and
    philosophical proofs, 54–57
religious discrimination, 81–82, 85.
    *See also* affirmative action
ritual, concept of, 64–66
Robinson, John A. T., 70
R-statement, 25–32
Russell, Bertrand, 75, 117
Russian government, 82

## S

Samkhya, Hinduism, 64
Santayana, George, 75
Schilpp, Paul Arthur, 75
Schleirmacher, Friedrich, 34
scientific method, 83–84, 100
Shmarb, John, 121–25
skepticism, 53
Socrates, 41
soft determinism. *See* determinism and freedom
Spanish Inquisition, 69
Spinoza, Baruch, 69
St. Augustine, 33, 34, 75
Stebbing, L. Susan, 9–10, 13
stereotypical thinking, 88
Stilpo, 32
St. John's College, 97
Stoic school, 53
Stoppard, Tom, 47
*The Strange Case of John Shmarb: An Aesthetic Puzzle* (Cahn and Griffel), 121–25
Stravinsky, Igor, 123
supernaturalistic religion, 64–71
superstition, 65–66
symbolism, 67

## T

Talisse, Robert B., 110
tasks, mindless vs. meaningful, 112
Taurasi, Diana, 98
Taylor, Richard, 25, 31, 32
teacher, claims for effective, 93–96
    intellectual perspective, 93, 94–95
    role model, 93, 95
    teaching effectiveness, 93–94
technology and capitalism, 82
teleological argument, 48–53
theism. *See* God
theism, traditional. *See* religious belief
theodicy project, 58–63
theological dogmatism, 47–53
    empirical evidence, 47–53
    reason and Christianity, 47–53
    truth of traditional Christian theology, 47–53
theology, independent of morality, 46
Theravada Buddhism, 64
*Theory of Valuation* (Dewey), 76, 77–78
Thomson, Judith Jarvis, 93n11
time, 25–32
*Times* (of London), 89–90
Torah, 37
de Torquemada, Tomás, 69
totalitarianism, 82
traditional education. *See* education
true
    future statement, 31–32, 36
    R-statement, 25–32
truth, 25–32
*The Tyranny of Testing* (Hoffman), 89–90

# Index

## U

underutilization, concept of, 87
universe, purpose of, 51
University of Michigan, 3
U.S. Department of Labor, 86

## V

Vienna Circle, 76
Vienna University, 76
Vitrano, Christine, 108
vocational education, 99

## W

Wallace, David Foster, 32
well-being
    death, how to view, 115–17
    happiness and ignorance, 105–7
    maximizing—, 108–10
    meaningful lives, 111–14
Whitehead, Alfred North, 75
Wiggins, David, 111
Wolf, Susan, 111–13

## Y

Yale College, 85n1

www.ingramcontent.com/pod-product-compliance
Lightning Source LLC
Chambersburg PA
CBHW070448090426
42735CB00012B/2490